CH00858424

WILL YOU TAKE THE DOGS OR THE DIAMONDS?

An Historical Account of a Very Eccentric Family

Anna Rains

authorHOUSE®

AuthorHouse™ UK Ltd.
500 Avebury Boulevard
Central Milton Keynes, MK9 2BE
www.authorhouse.co.uk
Phone: 08001974150

First published by AuthorHouse 7/28/2009

ISBN: 978-1-4389-8282-3 (sc)

Front cover blue bus reproduced with kind permission
of Aire Valley Transport Group, Bradford.

This book is printed on acid-free paper.

This book is dedicated to the future generations of the Holmes family, in the hopes it will give them understanding and information about their forebears.

I have found it fascinating to write and can only hope that the readers will enjoy it as much as I have done.

Acknowledgements

Michael Rains, my kind husband who patiently put up with me working on this book while in the middle of a difficult house move. Thank you to my sister-in-law, Vicky Holmes, who provided information about my brother and their family, and my sister Jo, who reminded me of old family stories. Janet Payne, my Godmother who told me about my parents and how they met. Edward Spratt, our neighbour, who spent many hours reading and editing my manuscript. Jenny Stevens, Melzie's 'other granny' who provided me with information about my father's family. Thanks to Gavin and Ginny Hogge for telling me about my brother's life in London and Ian Barron for his suggestions.

A very special thank you to David Murphy of The Royal Scots Regimental Museum, Edinburgh Castle who sent me masses of information about my grandfather, Lt Col David Aubrey Callender and my uncle Lt Col Hugo Callender.

Thank you to L Cpl Gorman of the Scots Guards for information about my uncle Capt Richard Aubrey Callender, who was also responsible for compiling most of the family trees. Without all of you this book would never have been written.

I would like to apologise in advance for any mistakes, either memory or spelling that may be contained in my manuscript - they are unintentional.

Contents

Acknowledgements   vii

Appendix   xi

Chapter 1 The Beginning Of The Holmes Family   1

Chapter 2 Mostly About The Callenders   7

Chapter 3 Jan's Letter   25

Chapter 4 Sussex And Wales Again   28

Chapter 5 Scotland   36

Chapter 6 Back To Sussex   40

Chapter 7 Eastbourne   53

Chapter 8 Hugo – 29th February 1944 – October 1995   65

Chapter 9 Edinburgh And Athol Crescent   74

Chapter 10 Hong Kong   82

Chapter 11 Back In England   112

Chapter 12 Laguna Niguel - 1969   123

Chapter 13 Mission Viejo - 1974   145

Chapter 14 Mission Viejo Again   159

Chapter 15 Return To England, 1981   165

Chapter 16 Cheshire 1983   174

Chapter 17whistler And Diana   196

Chapter 18 An Update On Our Lives   201

Appendix I   205

Appendix Ii   206

Appendix Iii   212

Appendix Iv   214

Appendix V   217

Appendix Vi   219

Appendix Vii   226

Appendix Viii   230

Appendix Ix   232

Appendix X   235

Appendix Xi   237

Appendix Xii   239

Appendix Xiii   240

Appendix Xiv   242

Appendix Xv   244

About The Author   249

APPENDIX

I   Information about Col. David
Aubrey Callender CMG

II   The Royal Scots – War Diary -
April 1915 – from the trenches

III   1st Battalion, The Royal Scots
1916 in the Field – Hortackoi

IV   Obituary of Lt Col. D.I.H.
Callender

V   Military Career of Capt.
Richard A Callender

VI   William Romaine Callender MP

VII   Records of the Family Romaine

VIII Peter Wright, gent.

IX   Lineage of the Wrights -
Children – great grandchildren

X.   Lineage 1 – Dermot MacMurrough

XI   Lineage II – Robert the Bruce

XII   Lineage 3 – William the Conqueror

XIII   Lineage 4 – King Robert

XIV   Linage – The Royal House of
       Stewart

XV   Lineage of the Lochinvar Family

CHAPTER 1

THE BEGINNING OF THE HOLMES FAMILY

London 1942

What an extraordinary life we have had, coming from such a diverse background. My mother, Hyacinth Angela Daphne, was born to a well to do Scottish family, landed gentry really, while my father, Alfred Douglas Holmes, came from the east end of London, a cockney or so he always said. My grandfathers were also at opposite ends of the pole. Colonel David Aubrey Callender CMG, a former member of the Royal Scots regiment had travelled extensively, while my father's father was a 'toy salesman', a barrow boy my sister and I always joked. We learned much later that my father had been married before and there were children from that wedding; however my father always denied they were his. He said he had married the lady to avoid a scandal for his older, married brother.

I was born in London during the blitz in the St Pancreas area on September 15th 1942 at 1.30 am. At the time my father was working as a fire-watcher, looking out for fires caused by the bombing and my mother had been working as a Voluntary Ambulance Driver. She had also worked at Waterloo Station, probably as a VAD.

We evacuated to Llandrindod Wales when I was three weeks old and moved into digs with a lovely family, the Mostyns. I understand that my early cot was a drawer pulled out of the bedroom chest and when I became too big for it I slept in an old wicker theatrical skip. Not that I remember.

I am not sure why we moved so often but it may have had to do with a family secret that I only heard about when I was twenty one years of age, but more of that later.

Meeting between my Mother and Father

My parents met on a small boat crossing over to one of the Scottish west coast islands shortly after World War II broke out. They were both working for ENSA, a variety group who entertained during the Second World War. My mother was very sick during the crossing and my father held a bowl for her to be sick into. Mother always said later that any man willing to do that was worth holding on to!

A lovely story from that era was one told by mother about acting in the pantomime 'Dick Whittington'. During the play, Dick's Cat has a big fight with the King Rat. At the end of the battle, which took place in a blackout, the Cat was supposed to kill the Rat, and when the lights came back up, the cat was to be seen sitting in the middle of the stage with the rat's tail in his mouth. In order to facilitate this, the tail was pinned on with a huge safety pin so that it could be undone during the blackout. Mother, for some reason did not know this and upon seeing the pin on the rat's costume, she thought, 'how untidy' and proceeded to stitch it very firmly in place. The lights dimmed and the fight went on and on while the Cat and the Rat tried to tear the tail off, muttering rude comments about the stupid *idiot* who'd done it! Needless to say mother was severely ticked off and made to unpick her careful sewing.

My Scottish grandmother heartily loathed my father and immediately cut off the financial allowance my mother had enjoyed over the years. We were very, very poor.

Before the war my father had been a musician, playing the French horn with several well known orchestras but by now his health was already failing and so he made a little money repairing wirelesses and doing other odd jobs.

He said he'd been with the BBC Symphony Orchestra and the London Philharmonic and used to make us laugh with a story about Sir Henry Wood. Apparently, on one occasion Sir Henry was conducting, with my father starting the concert with a horn solo. He began with the opening notes, only to be stopped as guilty latecomers crept into their seats. Three times Sir Henry made him stop and start again for other tardy newcomers and only when everyone was finally in their seats did the concert go ahead.

Years later my brother Hugo, a year and a half younger than me, wanted to learn to play my father's old fashioned horn. It had stops which you pushed in rather than the modern horn that has levers you press down on. I remember him coming in from school on a Friday afternoon, asking my father if he could teach him and then saying he'd got to know the Mozart Horn Concerto by Monday!

He didn't just play the French horn in the orchestra but, when necessary, other instruments as well. During one concert my father was asked to play a few notes on the triangle, as there were no horn parts in the musical score being played. At the time, and because the orchestra moved from place to place, he had neither the money or the time to get proper white dress shirts laundered and so, like many other members, he wore stiff paper shirt fronts. These were also useful for tearing bits off the bottom and writing notes on them. During the concert with the triangle my father was so busy writing a note to a friend in the orchestra (it was probably an arrangement to meet at the pub later) that he missed his cue to play the three notes. He was severely ticked off by the conductor for *that* lapse of concentration.

In between his musical responsibilities my father turned his hand to many things, including, when he was quite young, helping one brother in his barber's shop. It didn't last long after he accidentally cut a big chunk of one side of a very fine pair of moustaches. (My father was always shooting a line, so we were never sure whether this story was true or not!) He also worked in a garage and later in an electrical shop, which helped him when we lived in Llandrindod Wells.

Then there was the time when he drove a baker's van. His first marriage was a distant memory, although he didn't get a divorce until many years later, he was taking an attractive young woman to the pictures. She had told her parents he was a famous musician but when he turned up in his boss's, rather tatty van, full of bread ready for the next day's delivery, the romance came to a rapid end.

He became, for a short time, a door to door salesman. I am not sure what he was selling but I do know it gave him a lifelong hatred of higher purchase, and borrowing money instead of saving to pay outright for the goods.

I will probably repeat my self somewhere, but my father was the kindest, most generous, spiritual, and the least malicious man I have ever come across. I feel very privileged to have been his daughter. I am very glad I seem to have inherited some of his very high beliefs.

Llandrindod Wells

We stayed in Llandrindod Wells for the duration of the war. My brother Hugo Christopher was born on February 29th 1944. When he arrived he had masses of black hair, mother took one look at him and said that she wasn't expecting a spaniel puppy, much to the midwife's disgust.

My sister, Winifred Elaine Daphne was born on September 6th 1946. She hated the Winifred and the Daphne and was called Elaine, or Blossom as my mother often referred to her. This lasted until some years later when we were back in Wales, she climbed out of the stream running through the garden covered in mud from head to toe. My mother addressed her as Blossom and she replied, "I ain't Blossom, I's Jo Jo!" She has remained Jo to the day she died.

I don't remember much about those early years and I certainly do recall being told about the time when some wild young Canadian soldiers, who were camped near Llandrindod Wells, went round the town handing out bars of chocolate from their rations, to all the babies and small children left in their prams outside various shops. Naturally there were some very messy children awaiting their mothers. One or two were furious at the sight of their chocolaty infants, much to the amusement of the young men who were hiding round corners to watch the mothers re-appear.

Mother used to tell us about the time she sent Daddy to buy some sugar and he came back with a piano accordion. He couldn't resist it as it was such a good deal! Mother was not too pleased.

The winter of 1947 was awful. Snow up to the top of the hedgerows and with my father's health getting worse, my parents decided to move to Sussex. Unfortunately we didn't have any money. However a lovely gypsy family living next door to us came to our rescue. Their name was Egerton and they were well known as being the richest family in Llandrindod Wells. They suggested we bought a bus and then helped us fit it out with pre-war curtains and furniture.

The men were market gardeners, while their women took in laundry. 'Old Ma Egerton' was exactly like the grandmother in the book 'Cold Comfort Farm'; she was a terror. At intervals she would suddenly decide she could not bear living in a house any longer and retire to her caravan. This was the most beautiful caravan I have ever seen. Inside it was completely panelled with richly inlaid and ornate mahogany. The furniture was made of this beautiful wood and all the utensils were silver. She had heavy thick red velvet curtains, which she afterwards gave to us. Outside it was a real horse drawn gypsy wagon.

The entire family, about twenty of them altogether, lived in one house. Downstairs was the dingy little laundry. Upstairs you could not move because they had converted all their money into 'portable property' In other words the whole place was thick with silver and gold jugs, teapots, dishes, vases, saltcellars and everything else imaginable on equally beautiful Georgian tables and chairs. But there wasn't a book in the house as none of them could read.

I was about eight when I, and most of us in the class at school, were all detailed to try and teach Harold, their youngest son, how to read, but he was determined not to. Harold, at the age of thirteen was still in primary school, not because he was stupid because he certainly wasn't, but because he flatly refused to learn anything. He would bring sweets to school to bribe us with to read to him and of course we were willing to be bribed. The teachers were at the stage where they just shrugged their shoulders and let him get away with it.

Living in the Bus

Bus equipped, we set off to drive across country towards Sussex only to discover very rapidly that we were not allowed just to stop and park anywhere. The police would move us on, thinking we were either gypsies or tinkers. The only way round this was to get a 'showman's license' which we eventually did. To begin with we drove to Porthcawl and joined the funfair there. My mother ran the Hoop-la stall and my father said he was the attendant outside the 'fat lady's' tent.

After a few months there we joined Sanger's Circus as 'fly-posters'. I still have memories of that time. We would go out at night, Mother driving the bus, while daddy, with the bucket of paste, me with the brush and my brother clutching the poster climbed out to stick up one of the circus posters illegally. Why the night? Because the posters were always put up on somebody's tree or fence and we always hoped that by the time they found the poster the paste would have dried and difficult to remove. We obtained our 'showman's license' and continued to Sussex where we found a piece of land near Peacehaven.

I must say I never expected to meet up with anyone from that period of my life, however, about forty years later, when helping with an NSPCC fund raising event in Prestbury, Cheshire, I did meet up with someone. At the evening wine and supper party I began talking to the accordionist who was entertaining us for the evening.

"I'm not really a musician, I'm actually circus folk," he said.

"That's really interesting! We once worked with a circus, Sanger's Circus." I replied.

"George Sanger – he was my uncle!"

"My parents were really friendly with the lion tamer and his wife," I added.

"My Uncle Bert and Auntie Freda!"

He was almost exactly the same age as my brother Hugo and so, although I did not remember him, we must have played together as children. What a small world!

Years later when my sister was asked where she was born, she replied: "I was born in a bus, but the bus moved on." This wasn't actually true, but she wasn't very old when we set off in the bus.

CHAPTER 2
MOSTLY ABOUT THE CALLENDERS

The Background to Both my Families Parent's

It is perhaps appropriate to explain my parent's backgrounds further at this stage.

Of my father's I know little. He was born on February 7th 1896. His grandmother, Matilda Augusta Snell, born in 1828, was a much married lady. Her first husband was John William Hatch from Cornwall and she had at least four children by him, but by 1871 she was married to Samuel D Holmes who was born in 1820 and had another four children by him, including my grandfather Samuel Brent Holmes. In 1881 she was married to Alexander Andrade and was living in Barking, Essex with him and three of her children, Sydney, Samuel and Matilda Holmes. Sydney, my grandfather was born in Hackney in 1869 and in 1881 went with an elder brother and sister to live in Barking with their father and stepmother. His mother, my grandmother, was Emily Charlotte Holmes, (nee Giles) of 15 John's Road, West Hackney. We understand he was one of a large family.

Daddy said he'd joined the army when he was thirteen and became a boy trumpeter. He also told us his parents were musicians and travelled extensively! It came as a complete surprise when, requesting his birth certificate, to discover his father had been a toy salesman. I do know that he was wounded during the war as he had the scar from a bullet on the side of his neck. After that I know very little, and am not sure how many of his stories are really true, until he met my mother.

They were also very different to look at. My father, as I remember him was about five feet five while mother was five feet eight. Daddy was well built, or even quite stout! Mother was always fairly slim and very beautiful as a young woman. She was the outgoing one while my father was ill for most of the time I sadly remember. He suffered from emphysema accentuated by playing the French horn and smoking hand rolled cigarettes.

Mother's Family

My mother was a direct descendant of nine kings and queens of Scotland, Ireland, William the Conqueror, and included such illustrious persons as Robert the Bruce, James I and young Lochinvar.

She was born in Edinburgh, at her grandmother's house, on February 11th 1908, the third child of my grandparents, Lt. Colonel David Aubrey Callender CMG, (11th November 1868 – 7th October 1953), of The Royal Scots, the Royal Regiment and Violet Moncrieff Lockhart Wright Callender, (- 24th February 1953). My grandfather met my grandmother on the doorstep of her home when she was fifteen and fell in love with her but had to wait seven years before they married on 6th June 1900.

Mother had a privileged upbringing, being taken to India in 1909 where she remained until 1911when she returned to England before going back to India in 1913 for a year, while my grandfather was stationed there. According to my sister, my grandparents came back from India because grandmother was rather flirtatious and was about to cause a scandal in the Regiment!

On one occasion when my mother was returning to India for a visit she shared a cabin with Lawrence of Arabia's mother.

The family then mostly lived in Eastbourne from 1914 – 1933 before moving to Birnam, outside Dunkeld in Scotland.

My great grandparents lived in Edinburgh in one of the large houses. Backing on to the end of the garden was another house where my great grandfather's mistress lived. He would announce he was going out to smoke a cigar, but it was really a signal that he was off to climb over the wall at the end of the garden to visit his mistress!

I believe that my great grandparents, on my grandmother's side, rented the large country house, Cardrona, near Peebles. It was built around 1840. Mother used to talk about how much they loved it. I am not sure if the old house is still there but there is a grand hotel and golf complex in the village.

We were always told that great, great grandfather had been one of the founder members of the Royal Bank of Scotland. Many years later, when staying with Aunt Nathalie, I went into the main branch on Princess Street. The head cashier glided towards my aunt and me and dealt with our business himself. I was astonished by this as my allowance was only £4 per week for rent, food and everything, but aunt Nathalie said that he still recognised 'one of the family' which was why he was so attentive.

My mother had two brothers and one sister, Richard Aubrey who was seven years older, Winifred Nathalie Maud Yolande, four years older and a younger brother David Ivan Hugo. (My sister insisted that both my uncle and my brother Hugo were named after one of my great grandmother's favourite carriage horses.)

One of mother's earliest memories of Aunt Nathalie, one of those people who contradicted everything and everybody, was when mother crept up behind her with the biggest book she could manage and hit her over the back of her head!

Lieutenant Colonel David Aubrey Callender, CMG

(I think it is appropriate to add the information here that was sent to me by David Murphy of The Royal Scots Museum in Edinburgh.)

Born: 11 November 1868

Lt. Col. D.A. Callender was appointed 2nd Lieutenant in The Royal Scots on 14th September 1887 and joined the 1st Battalion at York.

He was promoted to Lieutenant on 23rd January 1890.

On 7th March 1892 he joined the 2nd Battalion at Malta who were embarking on board the transport ship SS *Avoca* bound for India. According to entries in the newly published Regimental magazine *The Thistle*, he acquitted himself well in the field of training and in the other major pastimes of the garrison town of Wellington, Madras, which were cricket, football and gymkhana.

In March 1893 he returned to the U.K. for a spell of duty at the Regimental Depot at Glencorse, near Penicuik, which was responsible for training new recruits and then sending them to one of the two Regular battalions. He took one such draft to the 1st Battalion at York in October 1893.

Lt. Callender rejoined the 2nd Battalion in India in 1895 as they were about to leave the garrison town of Belgaum for Berma.

He was promoted to Captain on 7th April 1896. On promotion he took over command of H Company, however a period of ill health meant he spent some time recuperating in Ceylon. Another bout of extended medical leave between October 1897 and January 1898 occurred before his return to the U.K. He returned to Edinburgh in February 1898 to take up the post of Adjutant of the 4th Volunteer Battalion, Royal Scots, which later became the 6th Battalion under the Territorial Force reforms. During his stay in the city he became Treasurer of the Regimental Association, a position he held until 1912. His time with the volunteers ended in 1904 when he joined the 1st Battalion at Blackdown. It was during this period he was presented to H.R.H. King Edward VII at a levee held by the Battalion.

Promotion to Major occurred on 16th November 1904.

In 1905 the 1st Battalion moved to Shorncliffe, Kent, then in March 1907 Major Callender took his leave of them once again and moved north to take command of the Depot for two years. It was during this time there that Mrs Callender gave birth to a girl on 11th February 1908, (my mother). In 1909 he returned to the 1st Battalion as they prepared to depart for India where they met the 2nd Battalion in Bombay as they returned home, the first time the two Battalions had met since the Crimean War. The 1st Battalion then moved up country to garrison duties at Bareilly. His stay was brief and he returned to the U.K. the following year and was with the 2nd Battalion at Barry in May 1910. The 2nd Battalion was presented with new colours on 20th July 1911 and Major Callender's part in the ceremony was described in the next edition of *The Thistle*. (See appendix at end.)

On his promotion, on 6th August 1912, Lt. Col. Callender was appointed Commanding Officer of the 1st Battalion and sailed once again for India on 18th September 1912 and took up his new post on 14th October at Allahabad. After the outbreak of the war the 1st Battalion were recalled home arriving at Winchester on 20th November 1914. Their stay was a short one as they had to be re-equipped and cross the Channel to France by the 20th December. Further training was carried out at Aire before they went into the line south of Ypres in January 1915. The Battalion quickly learnt to adapt to the routine of trench warfare – holding the front line, being relieved, resting, providing working parties, relieving and into the front line again. Their first major action was at St. Eloi on 14th/15th March 1915, this was followed by the 2nd Battle of Ypres from mid April to late May and although not involved in the worst of the fighting, they sustained 341 casualties. (See the extracts of the War Diary in the appendix.) It was during this period of fighting that he was 'Mentioned in Dispatches'. The 1st Battalion remained in the Ypres sector until November 1915 when they moved to Marseille and embarked for the Balkans and Salonika, a little known theatre of the First War. The Battalion had arrived there on 13th February 1916 and spent most of their war in the Struma Valley fighting against the Bulgarians. On 6th August Lt. Col. Callender's tour of duty with the Battalion came to an end and it is assumed he returned to the U.K. Army lists of the period show he took command of one of the new Labour Corps units from 13th April 1917, possibly the 34th Labour Battalion and remained with the Labour Corps until the end of the war.

He went on 'Retired pay' on 7th January 1920.

Lt. Col. Callender's medals, which are held in the Regimental Museum, (Accession Nos. 1428 to 1431) are *Companion, The Most Distinguished Order of St Michael and St George* (CMG), *1914-15 Star, British War Medal, Victory Medal* with 'Mentioned in Dispatches' oak leaves.

He attended the Presentation of Colours to the 2nd Battalion on 29 November 1948 and watched his son, Hugo, perform the same duties he had carried out at the previous Presentation of Colours in 1911.

While my grandfather and Uncle Hugo were in The Royal Scots, Uncle Dick joined the Scots Guards. At some point Uncle Dick added one of his grandmother's names and became Capt. R.A. Morison-Callender.

Obituary of Lieutenant Colonel D.A. Callender CMG
'Eheu fugaces, Postume, Postume, Labuntur anni.....'

(I have decided to put this in here rather than at the end of the book as it sheds more light on his career. It is from *The Thistle,* November 1954.)

To those accustomed to the use of Latin in their daily converse this might be freely translated in the Scottish tongue as 'Michty me, hoo the years gang by.'

The above preamble occurs to me when I try to write of Colonel David Aubrey Callender, my old friend and brother officer. There will be few now who can remember this true and faithful Royal who looked upon the Regiment as his home, and who never wanted anything else. One of the real Regimental officers who formed the backbone of the old Army.

Like all of us he had to answer the summons of old Father Time with his scythe. 'Death and Mess Bills', as we used to say, get us all in the end. I hope 'Taffy', as we called him, had a peaceful passing, for he deserved it. (I couldn't find out why they called him Taffy – *the author*)

I first met him in 1891 in York where, after Zululand and Natal, the 1st Battalion was stationed. After a few months there Callender was ordered to command a draft sailing to join the 2nd Battalion in Malta. Another subaltern and I accompanied him. The only trouble we had *en route* was a pub at Victoria Station. This pub had two doors, and as soon as we got the men out through one door they re-entered by the other.

And so to Bombay, where we trans-shipped to a trooper of the Indian Marine, arriving in due course at Cannanore where disembarked. Incidentally, the Commanding Officer's helmet fell in the sea here causing much indecent mirth. Callender and I carried the Colours up the Ghats to Wellington, where he and I shared a bungalow and very happy we were.

Years later in the 1914-18 war in France he was commanding the 1st Battalion which crossed from India, and I was commanding the 2nd

Battalion which had crossed to France from Plymouth in 1914. We met on a road in Belgium. I can see him now riding in front of his Battalion while I with the 2nd Battalion lined the road and cheered.

Apart from a relief in the trenches, that I think was the last occasion on which we met. Later he went with the 1st Battalion to Macedonia.

Much of what I have written may seem somewhat out of place in an obituary notice, but I hope it may be of interest to any old Royals who chance to read it. I hope too, that it may be of some interest and help to younger Royals. They may perhaps gather from it something of that feeling of pride and glory which comes to all who serve in the 1st Foot, with its long history and fine traditions. To them Colonel Callender should be an example, God rest his soul. F.J.D. (Writer of the Obituary)

More about the Family

The family lived in Eastbourne from 1914 until 1933 when they moved to Scotland.

Mother attended St Winifred's school, a day school, while Aunt Nathalie was sent off to boarding school. The sad thing was that my mother would have loved to have gone away to school and my aunt hated it and was very jealous that mother was kept at home.

My mother was a woman who was an intellectual with a brilliant brain – and not much practical sense, or at least with little inclination to do any housework and certainly her cooking left a great deal to be desired! In fact when she took her final exams at St Winifred's she took eleven papers and got distinction in ten of them and excellent in the 11th. Unfortunately my grandmother wouldn't permit her to go to Oxford or Cambridge 'as girls of her class did not do that sort of thing'. It was a terrible waste of such an extraordinary brain. Mother would have made a wonderful politician or political wife. The family always hoped she would marry Lord Hailsham, or Quentin Hogg as he was at the time she and he went canvassing together for the Conservative party in the late 20's.

My mother told us a story about her parliamentary endeavours.

She and Quentin Hogg were doing the rounds and promoting the fact that a man leaving the army could look after his family on one acre of land. They could be fully sufficient with a cow, which could supply enough milk for them, land for vegetables, chickens and perhaps a goat and so on. When mother made an impassioned speech, an old farmer stood up and said that if anything was going to get him to change his voting habits away for the Tories, that one would have done, because in his opinion, it simply wasn't possible. Mother told him she had received the notes from Party headquarters. He said he would be interested to know how the Tories had arrived at the figures. Mother checked it out and found that all the experiments had been done at Kew Gardens with the very best of materials available. After that she was a little more circumspect about what she spoke about in public.

Mother married just once, although she was engaged to a Mr Botham-Wetham, but she broke that off when she decided she really couldn't bear to be called Mrs Bottom-Wettum! Aunt Nathalie never married; Uncle Hugo twice. His first wife, died in a very bad car crash when they were on their way to my brother, Hugo's, wedding. Uncle Hugo's second wife, Ros, had been a bridesmaid at his first. There were no children from the first marriage and so it was a big surprise when a son arrived from his second union.

Capt. Richard Aubrey Callender

Uncle Dick, who joined the Scots Guards, reached the rank of Captain before, we understand, he was invited to leave the Regiment. He was married three times but did not have any children, although his first wife was pregnant when he married her. It is alleged that his Colonel, a titled and already married, gentleman, was the father and Uncle Dick married her to avoid any scandal that might have occurred. Whether it was this that caused him to leave the army, or something else, we do not know.

My great grandparents set him up in Kenya where they bought him an estate, but several years later, having lost the property, he returned to England penniless, and without his wife and child. I am led to believe it cost the titled officer dearly throughout the rest of his life!

There is a comment in one of papers ruling on the family Trust and outlining the payments that – *'By the Deed of Alteration Mrs Wright cancelled the Purpose (fifth) of the original Trust Deed and* substituted *a liferent for the grandchildren,* (my mother, Aunt Nathalie and Uncle Hugo) *with the fee to pass to their issue (EXCEPTING THOSE OF MR RICHARD CALLENDER WHO HAD BY THEN OFFENDED HIS GRANDMOTHER).* (This was actually written in capital letters, so she must have been cross!)

His second wife was called Daphne and the third Kaye, a barmaid. They lived on a titled gentleman's estate for years.

During Uncle Dick's time in the Scots Guards, he told a story about being based at Windsor Castle during the reign of King George V and Queen Mary. Apparently despite her straight laced appearance, as soon as the King returned to London and Buckingham Palace, Queen Mary would throw wild parties and invite all the young officers! This could be apocryphal because one would never believe old Queen Mary was anything but totally straight laced.

(See appendix V for the Army Record of Captain R A Callender)

William Romaine Callender MP

It was many years later in about 1984, when I was living in Cheshire that Uncle Dick; (Richard Callender) mentioned my great, great uncle William Romaine Callender and told me about the bust of him in Manchester Town Hall. I went to look for it and sure enough there he was with a very fine pair of side whiskers. Judging by the amount of information concerning him, he was highly thought of. He was a very high ranking member of the Freemasons and did a great deal to establish the Conservative party constituency branches in the Lancashire and Cheshire areas.

It was the first time I learnt about the Manchester connection with our family. I also discovered that the main library in Manchester has a great many documents referring to him. I have included some of them in an appendix at the end of the book.

(See appendix VI, information about William Romaine Callender, and VII – The Records of the Family Romaine, which include a very early mention of the name Callender - under William Romaine, a merchant of Hartlepool, born 1672)

Birnam, Nr Dunkeld

My grandparents bought St Mary's Towers in Birnam, a small town near Dunkeld, in the thirties and the family lived there. When my husband and I went to look for it during the nineties, sadly the old house had been pulled down many years ago and modern houses built instead. Both my grandparents are buried in the churchyard at Birnam although they had lived in Perth for many years before their deaths.

Uncle Hugo's friend the Earl of Mar

Mother used to tell us stories about Uncle Hugo's best friend Jamie Lane, later the Earl of Mar. My grandmother was very anxious that my uncle Hugo should marry Jamie Lane's sister and to my everlasting annoyance handed over the family diamond tiara to her. We did once go and visit the Earl of Mar who lived in a small house in Station Road! He would attend the House of Lords so that he could claim his daily attendance allowance; otherwise he had very little money. He had his coronation robes on display in a glass case with the vague idea of inviting American tourists to his home and charging a fee to be photographed, either with them wearing the robes, or standing alongside him in his ermine and coronet! We all thought it was more likely to be white rabbit rather than ermine.

Early Girl Guiding

Life for her in the late 20's and thirties was one of idleness and socializing. The idleness didn't suit mother, she had so much energy.

She became involved with Scouting and was one of the first Girl Guides, although she was older than most of the others when she joined. Apparently a film was made to promote Guiding and mother acted in it. It must have taken a long time to film because mother said they filmed the beginning and the end before the middle. During the filming she contracted measles and a lot of her hair fell out and so the beginning and the end of the film showed her with a thick plait of hair, while in the middle her plait was very much thinner!

Before she went off to Guide camp, and coming from a family where she had never been expected to know anything about cooking, she descended into the kitchens to ask the cook to show her how to peel potatoes. She didn't want the other Guides, most of whom came from less exalted homes, to laugh at her.

Presentation at Court

At the end of the twenties, probably 1927, mother and Aunt Nathalie were both presented at the court of Queen Mary. The fashion was for short, knee length dresses, which they wore, but they still had to wear a long flowing lace train and had ostrich feathers in their hair. They looked like a couple of dripping candles! (There is a photograph of them in later on in the book). According to mother, Lady Mountbatten was in attendance that day and scandalised the court by wearing a very short skimpy and almost transparent, bright green dress.

Food in a Country House

I find it astonishing how much food they consumed in those days – and how she stayed so slim. Mother told us they would get up to a large cooked breakfast, including porridge served with salt and cream. No sugar or syrup ever topped mother's porridge in her entire life. Then would be a choice of kippers; smoked haddock; eggs; bacon; kidneys; mushrooms and so on with lashings of toast and marmalade. My grandfather used to say that the toast should be just thick enough to carry the butter and marmalade to the mouth!

Then they would have mid-morning coffee. A three course lunch was followed by afternoon tea with sandwiches, scones and cakes, and at about 8.00 o'clock they sat down to a five or six course dinner. Then, if they attended a ball, there would be a supper or breakfast of something like kedgeree at the end of the ball before leaving for home.

Social Life between the Wars

As they were living in Scotland, most of the balls would be mainly Scottish country dancing. I still have my mother's sash in the Morison tartan. It was tradition for the women to wear white with tartan sashes, but the men were the colourful ones in full Highland dress with many different tartans on display. Most men wore kilts, but The Royal Scots, The Royal Regiment, wear tartan trews, which distinguishes them from other regiments. Balls were held in the large country houses, many of them scattered at quite long distances from Dunkeld, although one of the closest was the Duke of Athol's home, Athol Palace. Mother later met up with him again when she was working as a nanny for Viscount Cowdray in Midhurst. They had amusing talks about the past.

The young men and women would think nothing of driving several hours to a dinner and ball. Mother once said that although they didn't know at that time there would be another World War, there was a sense, after the First World War, to have as much fun as possible. Tennis parties, picnics, shooting parties in the autumn, after the glorious 12th of August, when the shooting season began, were all part of the social season.

There was one story about a group of them, including some dashing young officers from my grandfather's regiment, The Royal Scots, drove to ball about three hours away. They were warned it could snow, but being young, they laughed and went anyway. Half way home they ran into a blizzard and the three cars were forced to come to a standstill. Not knowing quite what to do, they decided to make their way back to a house a few hundred yards back. The girls lifted up their long skirts and they trudged back through increasing drifts of snow. It was about five in the morning when the astonished owner, Mr Robbie McLeod, a local landowner, met them at the front door wearing his pyjamas. He had no other option but to invite them in. The weather became worse and they were stranded for three days, all of them still in their evening dress! As the owner played the bagpipes, they continued the ball each evening with Robbie playing reels and strathspeys. My grandmother was naturally very worried, but the electricity lines were down, mobile phones were a long way into the future and so they had no way of letting anyone know. However being young they all thoroughly enjoyed their adventure. I understand that the estate was well stocked with chickens and ducks, the pantry with food, and Mr McLeod's cellar contained plenty of wonderful wines and bottles of Malt Whisky so nobody felt deprived.

Another time, when several of the young officers were staying, my grandmother dragged them off to church. The minister, who was a strict Presbyterian, was preaching about St John versus Jezebel. Glaring at the young men he asked in a menacing voice,

"Who would you rather be with, St John, or with *that woman* Jezebel?"

The young officer answered him with a look at my mother, "You take St John, I'll have Jezebel!"

She told us another story about the time she was visiting friends in a country house near Aberdeen. A large group of friends were coming to stay for the Braemar Royal Highland Gathering. Everyone was roped in to help the staff make up beds. Mother was in a little used room and pulling up the sheets and blankets when she realised that something or someone on the other side of the bed was helping her – but there was nobody else in the room. Quickly finishing the bed, she fled to the Lady of the house, who laughed and said that there was a story about a long deceased former housekeeper who had been seen wandering the passages with a large bunch of keys. It was generally thought it was she who was still helping out.

Play Acting at Christmas

I think mother's love of theatre, acting, writing and production was cultivated while she was living at St Mary's Towers. During a Christmas and New Year visit of a number of my uncles' and mother's friends she decided to produce a play – it was loosely, in fact very loosely based on a combination of Noel Coward's two plays 'Blythe Spirit' and 'Hay Fever' and Shakespeare's 'Macbeth'. She didn't have enough members of the cast and so had to improvise! She also did not have the time to buy the original scripts – although she did have a copy of Macbeth, but didn't think suitable for a Christmas house party.

It began with a group of bohemian characters who were involved in emotional havoc among a houseful of visitors, combined with a ghost. Aunt Nathalie, who was playing the part of the ghost, and all three of Macbeth's witches, forgot her entrance and appeared at completely the wrong, and inappropriate, time. One of my uncle's friends, who was playing a female part, became so helpless with laughter that he came on, (like my son Sean did many years later) wearing a wig which he had accidentally put on backwards. Trying to find his way out of the hair covering his face, he managed to get some of the locks into his mouth and proceeded to try and speak his part while spitting out the offending hair. The audience were in complete hysterics, including my mother who was acting as stage manager, Lady Macbeth, several other smaller parts, prompt and anything else that needed to be done. Not sure she ever created quite so much mirth in any other production, but it certainly gave her a huge desire to go on to do lots of things connected with the stage and acting.

There was another time when two tiny nuns appeared at my grandmother's front door trying to sell exquisite handmade nightwear. They had a map of Scotland marked with castles and big houses. Unfortunately many of the castles were ruins and so mother got out her little bright red Baby Austin sports car and drove them round to sell to all her friends.

A story about my uncle Hugo, which may be untrue, was about his life at Sandhurst. Apparently, or so the story goes, Uncle Hugo and some of the other officer cadets, took great pride in tossing butter pats up on to the ceiling of the Mess, and wait until the room became warm enough for the butter to drip down on to some unfortunate young man's dress uniform! Never having visited Sandhurst I have no idea whether this is possible or not.

Rolls Royce

It is hard to imagine but mother was actually the least eccentric of the female members of her family.

Before the days of cars, my great grandmother kept special expensive peppermint chocolates especially for her carriage horses. The grandchildren were forbidden to touch them. The story goes that she owned the first Rolls Royce in Scotland, which was left to my uncle Hugo when she died, but as the family knew, he would probably wreck it, they secretly sold it and gave him the money instead. I don't think he ever forgave them.

My grandmother went out of her way to get herself noticed. She always had Rolls Royce's until the chauffeur retired, but would not drive very far in them as she was inclined to car sickness. On one occasion when the family was heading by train for Eastbourne for the summer, they arranged for the Inverness to London train to stop at Dunkeld – you could do that in those days! The chauffeur, George, drove them to the station where he assisted with the luggage. My grandmother waited until people put their heads out of the carriage windows to see why they were making an unscheduled stop and then drawing herself up to her five foot height said in an imperious voice, "George, meet us in Eastbourne," where upon poor George had to drive like a maniac to get there before them!

It was upon the retirement of her chauffeur that my grandmother, at the age of sixty-five learnt to drive and went everywhere at 70 miles per hour! Of course she never took a test as it wasn't necessary in those days.

On another famous occasion the family had taken two of the small first class compartments trains used to have and my grandmother, while standing on the platform in front of the audience of fellow travellers leaning out of the carriage windows, turned to my grandfather as asked in a very loud voice, "David, will you take the dogs or the diamonds?" Needless to say he got the dogs – pugs, my grandmother always had several.

My eccentric grandmother also loved seeing the reaction of

gentlemen wearing kilts. She would happily sit stirring her hot cup of tea or coffee until the spoon was red hot and then casually lean over, as if she was about to say something confidential, and place the hot spoon on the bare knee of the kilted gentleman and then roar with laughter when he jumped.

During one of their summer holidays in Eastbourne, my grandmother was standing outside the Grand Hotel saying goodbye to some friends when her knickers fell down. Without batting an eyelid, she simply stepped out of them and waved them to her departing friends!

That may have been one of the last times she went to the Grand. While walking past the back of the Hotel, she happened to glance down into the kitchen area. She was appalled to see a rather scruffy looking man, whose job was obviously to butter bread for afternoon tea. The weather was cool and the butter cold and he was finding it hard to smoothly butter the bread, and so she watched him put a lump of butter on the end of the knife and place it in his mouth where he breathed over it to warm it up! Feeling sick, and thinking about how many sandwiches she'd eaten at afternoon tea there, she tottered home and swore blind she would never enter the hotel again – and I believe she never did.

Bridge

My grandparents were very keen bridge players and my mother, who played regularly as well, insisted we learnt to play. I was thirteen, my brother eleven and Jo nine. I recall mother telling us that one day there would be three people who could and who wanted to play bridge and if we the fourth and couldn't, heaven help us. "You will learn" she added. I went on to play, but she completely put my brother and sister off for ever!

There are two lovely stories told by my grandmother. They may have been about the same silly old lady, but I don't know. The first one was when this lady picked up her hand and found it contained thirteen spades, all of them in fact. She then called the highest bid she could – a

22

grand slam in no trumps, not spades, and of course she never got in to play any of her spades.

The other story is about the time when the bidding went up and up, ending with a call of a grand slam in spades, (this means that you make all thirteen tricks, but in bridge you start counting from the sixth and so if you call seven spades it is the same as taking all the tricks). This little old lady suddenly said "Eight spades". She was admonished. "You can't call eight spades", they said.

"Why on earth not?" she asked.

"You can't call eight spades because you can't make it."

"Oh", she replied, "I often call things I can't make."

My Grandmother's Eastbourne Friends

Years later I met up with several of my grandmother's Eastbourne friends. One, a widow, Mrs Humphries-Davies, used to scare me. I once mentioned her former husband and was greeted with, in a very imperious voice, "Oh, my dear, he was eaten by a lion in Africa!" She had a stuffed lion's head fixed to the wall near the bathroom. It was sort of hidden round the corner of a dark corridor and so it always gave me a shock when I headed for the loo. I never dared ask if that was the offending lion!

I remember one evening when my parents attended one of Mrs H.D's famous *cocktail* parties. Mrs H.D. had invented her own cocktail – it consisted of neat gin topped up with Merrydown cider and was absolutely lethal. Mother, who had a notoriously weak head, drank several of these delightful concoctions. As she left Mrs H.D's house, she picked a huge bunch of daffodils from Mrs H.D's next door neighbour's garden, much to the fury of that neighbour. Upon arriving home she decided to make us omelettes for supper and proceeded to dish them up on upside down plates only to find them slide gracefully on to the floor!

Another lady, Mrs Ward, caused my brother Hugo to go into shrieks of mirth when she was explaining to my mother about her daughter's engagement. She said, "I just told Pamela that on her wedding night something *simply dreadful* will happen to you. Just lie back and take no notice – that's all I ever did". Small wonder Mrs Ward only had one daughter and her unfortunate husband died a few years after their marriage. Pamela listened to her advice and called off the wedding!

When Mrs Ward died, mother and her friend Mary went to the crematorium only to find they had arrived far too early (a habit of my mother's) and were at the wrong funeral! The deceased was a man and every thing said about him was totally impropriate for Mrs Ward. As they were sitting in the front row it was impossible to escape and they had a very difficult time trying to stifle the giggles all the way through.

My parents were as different as chalk and cheese – and yet my mother always said she would put my father first ahead of us children.

CHAPTER 3
JAN'S LETTER

(Author's note: Janet Payne was one of my mother's actress friends and later my Godmother.)

April 18 '05

My dear Anna,

I've been thinking – I will of course do the best I can, with a very ageing memory! But maybe Sandra could provide more and better fodder for you. (Sandra Payne, actress).

As for myself, my memories are rather sketchy I'm afraid. The annoying thing is that I kept a 5-year diary faithfully until November '39 when my brother died aged 31 and it was such a sad and difficult period for me and my parents who were under great stress. <u>But</u>, it was very shortly after that I first met, and was uplifted by your dear Mother!

I had been working in Rep at Theatre Royal Brighton and became friendly with a very nice Stage-Manager called Mary Leftwich. It was of course then war time and theatres were in a bad way but one actor had written a play and managed to get it put on in Croydon. He asked Mary to S.M. (stage manage), and she suggested a friend as Assistant. That of course was our Daphne who was then staying in digs in Wandsworth Common and as I was going to play in the thing, Mary asked her to meet me. I was still living with my parents in Clapham Common and one day Daphne walked from Wandsworth Common to Clapham Common! I can still recall what the effect it had on me and my parents at such a difficult time for us all and how she brought such a bright and encouraging uplift to us all, especially for my stricken father, a very anti-theatrical Victorian! who responded to her very bright and intelligent repartee and kindness. We forged ahead with the play and she was especially helpful to me and needless to say extremely efficient and always bright and smiling.

I can't remember how it all finished or what happened next. The war was then into the daily raids and bombings for months during which time I was working at the Air Ministry. Some time during this period, I discovered that Daphne was living in Kensington, I think, and I visited there to find that she had met Douggie and were together. I can only vaguely remember him, as always, very kind and sympathetic, and I particularly remember, I think, his wonderful eyes. He was, as I am sure you know, clairvoyant, and I shall never forget how uplifting it was that he sensed my brother (not knowing any details of his death) and how sincere he was and so very uplifting to me at that time. He had a most comforting and believable message for me which was a great help.

From then on, my memories are vague. I can only recall in the year of 1940 being in Rep at Llandrindod and in '42, I think, your parents suddenly appeared! They were living in a flat in town and I can remember visiting one day and can remember you sitting on a little chair – aged about two I think. Llandrindod was then a garrison town, given over to the training of Officer Cadets and we at the little theatre doing weekly Rep for mostly all the military! We formed a Theatre Club especially for them, inviting them to stay behind after the show for a sandwich etc., and then we took over an empty shop in the town and set up the Green Room Club just for them, where they could drop in and have coffee etc. and then Douggie took it over and ran it and arranged everything. I think he also did odd electrical jobs in the town.

After getting married in '43 I can only remember odd visits to you all in many and various parts of the country. One time I recall was somewhere in Wales in the middle of a field! I came on my own by coach which I think had to stop in the middle of nowhere to be met by you all trudging across acres, it seemed, of wet grass to get to the house, of which I can't remember much except that the loo was at the far end of the field, very rough, and which I didn't like at all. Hugo

26

I remember, about 5 or 6 was very boisterous and rather unrestrained and quite happily left to be so by your happily unaffected Mother!

Sometime later, Gil, Sandra and I visited you all somewhere in Sussex. By then you were all growing up and Sandra stayed with you in various places I think. Then of course came The Bus! And Mum wrote a book and then also a play on TV. I think I was just in it, somewhere around in it or some odd character which I can't recall.

Then there was another visit to a house near Eastbourne – I think you were working as a receptionist in a Hotel? I stayed a night at the Cavendish then Mum took me for a long, long tramp on the downs during which we had long conversations re our various problems! Family and otherwise – as usual she gave me much sound advice and always on the encouraging side…

I cannot remember much about your father. He was gentle and kind and I can't recall his last illness or death, when or where. Mum of course was always, in my memory, strong and amusing and always a great help to me and my problems. We corresponded a fair amount over the years and I do so miss her and wish she was still with us. She had such courage and energy and light-heartedness, at least that is how it appeared to me. And such courage. The last time Gil and I met her was at your kind arrangement I think, at the Rembrandt Hotel in Victoria where we met and chatted and had lunch and more chatter until the time ran out. I think you were coming to collect her? Can't remember. But I shall always have a picture of her, smiling and joking and always trying to encourage me to get a bit tougher! I remember her greatly when she was recounting an incident when her parents (in Scotland and good background?) were travelling, or moving to London and your aristocratic Grandmother called to your Grandfather, about to get on the train, "Will you take the birds or the diamonds?" Don't know why it has stuck with me, and the way your mum delivered it!

Till soon,
Fond memories,
Jan

CHAPTER 4
SUSSEX AND WALES AGAIN

Piddinghoe, near Peacehaven, Sussex

We travelled in our bus through Wales and England to the south coast where we bought a small piece of land, the idea being we would build a house there. My father's health was deteriorating and instead of a house we bought a caravan which we parked alongside the bus.

My memories of this period are limited but varied. I do know that my dislike of cooked spinach began at this time. Mother read somewhere that cooked stinging nettles taste exactly like spinach and are just as good for you. As we had an abundance of nettles in the 'garden' she filled a pot and cooked them. Unfortunately I knew they were stinging nettles!

Another memory is of my brother Hugo. He could have only been about three at the time. It was a lovely summer and my parents erected a small tent in the garden for Hugo and I to sleep in. (Not something anyone would do today!) One morning a neighbour came to tell my parents in a shocked voice that when he'd got up at about 5.30 am to go to work, he'd looked out of his bedroom window and seen my brother. The dew was still on the grass and covered the roof of the tent when the neighbour watched Hugo creep out of the tent, take off his pyjamas, climb up one side of the tent and slide down the other! Mother thought it was great fun and never stopped him.

The only doll I ever had dates back to the time we lived there. It was a black cloth doll and I loved her dearly, but I was always jealous of my sister Jo because she had a doll with lovely golden curls – at least she did until Hugo put a basin on her head and cut them all off. Curler, the name Jo gave her, was no longer curly!

We went to school in neighbouring Peacehaven and I remember walking back home across some very flat land and seeing a young bull chasing round a field with pony. The two of them came charging across the grass but while the pony turned away at the last moment, the bull couldn't stop and careered through the hedge and came to a grinding halt right in front of us. It was a pretty scary moment.

Back to Wales

I was seven when we returned to Wales and went to live on a desolate farm called the Rhonllywn on the edge of Radnor Forest. I never understood why it was called a forest because there were hardly any trees. Never very happy with horses, I became quite frightened of them because, on the forest, common land really, there were herds of Welsh mountain ponies running completely wild. They were very dangerous, especially on the occasions we had to venture out on to the common to fetch in horses and ponies that had broken out through insecure hedges. Gomer Ingram, the farmer, was very lazy, never getting out of bed until mid-morning. His cattle were milked at very odd hours – lunchtime and about ten o'clock at night. It was all hand milking of course.

We stayed in the main farmhouse to begin with. It was very primitive. No electricity, no running water and no proper sanitary arrangements. Potties under the beds, an outhouse with doors at either end - neither of which closed - and a two hole wooden seat comprised our lavatory. Pages torn out of the Farmer's Weekly were not as soft as the current Andrex toilet paper. Pigs or sheep grazing in the orchard behind the farmhouse would sometimes wander through the outside privy to reach the front garden. I remember that on either side of the path leading to this wondrous 'loo' were high box and privet hedges. To this day I loath the sweet sickly smell these bushes give off.

Baths were taken in a battered bath-sized tin bath placed in front of a roaring fire built in the old black range in the kitchen, with hanging kettle and oven to one side. Once a week was the ration for a bath, because it took too long to heat up the water for more frequent washing. Everyone bathed one after another in the same water!

Salted hams hung in the rafters above our heads, and the dairy was filled with hand made butter and cheese. Huge stone slabs covered the floor in the back kitchen, which made it a very cold room in the winter. The fireplaces in the bedrooms were the only form of central heating. We all huddled round the black iron range in the main kitchen, which was stoked up at night in order to keep it going non stop as it served as a heating, cooking and baking unit. I also remember the hardness of the stone hot water bottles we took up to bed at night.

Hilda Ingram, the farmer's wife seemed to be constantly baking. She would make bread, cakes and fruit tarts which we seemed to eat at all mealtimes regardless of whether it was breakfast, tea or lunch. Although there was still rationing we never seemed to go without anything – except chocolate. During the war the Canadians, who were camped nearby, would go round the farms and buy up all the eggs and butter they pleased. The black market thrived in this part of Wales.

On a wonderful occasion Hilda was standing in the yard chatting to a group of men when her goat wandered up to them. Walking behind Hilda it proceeded to start eating the back of her skirt. Unaware of what was actually happening, Hilda kept shooing the goat away. It was only when she turned away and the men gave a great shout of laughter she realised the goat had eaten its way to her waist line leaving a big hole and exposing her cammy knickers.

The Wern

Across a field on the farm there was an almost derelict cottage into which we moved. It was tiny. Two up and two down with absolutely no water, electricity or sanitation laid on. Downstairs was a kitchen and a living room and upstairs just the two bedrooms. Sandra Payne seemed to remember the Elsan lavatory sitting on the upstairs landing, but in my memory is was in a small shed outside near the back door.

Drinking water came from a spring across a field to which my parents took a bucket and placed it in the fresh water welling up from the spring and leave to fill itself every day. Sometimes the cattle would come along and knock the bucket over to the extreme annoyance of whichever parent had left it.

Washing water ran as a stream through the bottom of the patch that was supposedly a garden. The nearest main road was a mile away across fields over which we had to walk to school every day. On several occasions we were forced to turn round and take a different route when another local farmer stuck his huge Hereford bull in a huge open barn half way along path.

An old barn was built on to one end of the cottage into which Gomer Ingram stacked un-thrashed corn. Mice and rats moved in to enjoy the harvest but as their supply dwindled, and finally disappeared, they moved in with us, along with a fair supply of fleas. I still have strong memories of my father pealing back the bedclothes and catching the fleas on a damp piece of soap. Ughh – it continues to make me shudder!

I was given a pony, named Kitty, when I was about eight, and although she was tiny, I was always afraid of her, unlike my brother who would get on anything. Kitty was most unusual because she changed colour. In the summer her hair was almost black. In the middle of winter, it was almost white, and in spring and summer it went through the process of becoming darker or lighter.

The farmer put my brother up on an unbroken foal, but Hugo, who was fearless, didn't take long the get the pony used to him. We always rode bare back as we never had any saddles. The foal became very tame and used to come and stick its head through the cottage window and listen to the wireless. One day when the front and back doors were both open, and the three of us children were running through the house, mother heard a different noise and looked up to see the foal following us. On another occasion it also managed to climb half way up the very narrow staircase and had to be backed down.

Early School Days

Hugo and I attended the village school in Llandegly. It was run by the headmaster and his wife. A very posh title as the school only had about thirteen children there all together. It consisted of two rooms. One a proper classroom, but the infants were taught in what was really the cloakroom and in winter it was terribly unhealthy as wet raincoats and hats dripped water on to the floor all round them. There was also an open fire with no guard in front of it, something no school would be allowed today.

Mother had an awful falling out with these two when she discovered they were helping themselves to the children's meat rations. Most days we were given cheese pie and parsley sauce and in summer beetroot was added to the menu. I still dislike parsley sauce and beetroot! I clearly remember the row which took place outside the school. Mother accused them of stealing our meat and the headmaster's wife screamed like a fishwife, calling out to the other parents, "Look at this mad woman! She's mad you know!" I think the Welsh hatred of the English was certainly in force in that village. We were immediately taken out of the school and mother fought a battle with the local authorities to persuade them to send us to school in Llandrindod Wells.

Hugo and I travelled the eight miles each way every day. There was only one bus in and one out and so we were forced to wait after school until the bus came. Often we would use this time to do the shopping for mother. I was eight but my brother was only six at the time. On one occasion when my mother went into a shop in Llandrindod Wells for notepaper she was asked which sort. She replied that she didn't mind. "Oh, Mrs Holmes, your son is very fussy about what he buys," replied the shop keeper.

During the harvest we were all involved. The hay had to be turned by hand and then stacked loosely on to wooden hay carts drawn by huge shire horses. Hugo was even sent out on his own to do some ploughing when he was only about seven years old, again with horse drawn equipment.

We were happy although we had very little money. Mother wore gumboots for months as she couldn't afford to buy shoes. I have a mental picture of my mother wearing a headscarf fastened tightly round her head and tied at the front. She also wore a flowery overall and Wellington boots.

It was in the cottage that my father taught Hugo and me how to play chess and he attempted to teach me how to play the cello. He succeeded with chess but failed miserably with the musical instrument!

It is strange really that we all seemed to take after mother who was tone deaf, or so she said, and none of us could sing in tune. However the musical side jumped a generation as most of daddy's grandchildren became really good musicians.

I remember my eighth birthday. We had invited a number of children from Llandrindod Wells to come out to the cottage on the farm. They had to come for the entire day because of the bus situation and of course nobody had a car. We were too poor to have proper drinking glasses, but mother washed out jam jars for us. One of the Mostyn girls earnestly told us later that when she wrote an essay on the best thing that had happened that summer, she'd described the party but added, "I didn't mentioned the jam jars!"

Having almost no money we relied on the land and my father became very proficient at snaring rabbits with a wire snare. I think we ate so much rabbit stew, that and mixymatosis, which almost wiped out the rabbit population, put me off eating rabbit for life.

Sadly we lost our mongrel dog, Derry, when I was about eight. He began sheep worrying and had to be shot. There was nothing else to do as you cannot stop dogs when they start that.

We almost lost our cottage as well. One night there was a huge electrical storm during which a lightening strike hit the tree only yards from the front door. The storm not only brought down an enormous branch, but set the tree on fire as well. Fortunately, the weather turned into torrential rains which put the flames out. We were awfully close to it and for a long time, we were all terrified of thunder.

Sandra Payne - Actress

Also during that time an old friend of my mother's came from London with her daughter Sandra to visit. Janet Payne was the actress friend, who wrote the letter in a previous chapter, and years later her daughter joined the same profession. Coming from a much more civilised background, Sandra was always clean and nicely dressed, whereas we ran wild and were generally pretty muddy and dirty. Walking up from the cottage to the farmhouse to have tea with the

Ingram's, mother overheard my sister Jo encouraging Sandra to 'jump in it'. When she glanced over her shoulder Sandra was standing by a huge fresh cowpat just about to 'jump in it' with her nice tidy shoes. Mother kept Jan talking to distract her from stopping her daughter in what mother thought was what Sandra needed – a bit of good clean farm muck!

After leaving the Italia Conti Theatrical School, Sandra went on to work on the stage and television. She was in 'The Mousetrap' for a while, before going into television and sit-coms like 'Waiting for God', in which she brilliantly played the inebriated daughter-in-law, and Christine Harris in 'Triangle'. In fact when Sandra Payne actress, is 'googled' there are so many references it would take ages to read them all.

She was married three times. Her second husband was Alan Jay Lerner, of My Fair Lady fame, and they were married from 1974 - 76. She was the sixth of his eight wives. The third was Roy Boulting, one of the Boulting brothers. She married him after he and Hayley Mills divorced. They were married from 1979 – 1983. I remember she brought him to my sister Jo's wedding.

At some point during this time we acquired and old London taxi and thus became more mobile. My parents became involved with the elections and went out canvassing for the local M.P., one Desmond Donnelly. One evening we went to a political meeting and on the way home the fog was so bad, and with no 'cats eyes' in those days, my father walked in front of the vehicle with a torch to show mother, who was driving, where the edge of the road was. It took us ages to get home.

By this time my grandmother, now living in Perth in Scotland, was becoming very frail and mother decided we should move nearer to her. Mother had become reconciled with her parents prior to our move north when she took Jo and me up to stay with them in Pitlochry. We joined them at the Green Park Hotel for a week. Mother had made, all by hand, long evening dresses for us. They were dark blue and we felt very grown up when we went down for dinner in the evenings. While there, we were given the names 'Miss Nosy' and 'Miss Parker' as we were curious about everything – not unnaturally as the hotel was so different from our home in Wales. We were fascinated by the bathrooms in particular.

So, at the ages of nine, seven and five we moved house and schools yet again from Wales to Scotland.

CHAPTER 5
SCOTLAND

Errol, Perthshire

The house in the village of Errol, outside Perth, was a much more conventional. It was terraced with the front door opening right on to the main street - and with a resident ghost. Not that we children were aware of anything, but my father, who was very psychic, often felt an elderly couple pass through the house and out by the front door.

We stayed in Errol for about a year and a half – until after my grandparent's deaths. I was taken to visit them regularly and have a clear vision of sitting on their hairy white rug in front of the fire playing with a set of hounds, horses and a fox. They were tiny and sometimes I lost one or two in amongst the long fur.

While living in Errol I joined the Brownies and was very keen. My sister became a Brownie later on, by which time I was a Sixer. Poor Jo - I was responsible for teaching her how to tie knots and other Brownie skills. She was totally uninterested and so I tied her to a chair with her belt and forced her to listen to me! She refused to come any more after that and forcefully declined joining the Girl Guides later when we were back in Sussex.

The village school was rather unpleasant as they still had corporal punishment in those days. One very sadistic female teacher was enthusiastic about getting out the split leather strap and whacking you across the palm of your hand for the slightest reason. A girl in our class was always in trouble and I felt very angry on one occasion, when this teacher got out the belt because Lizzie's hands were stained with walnut juice. She explained that her mother had insisted on her peeling the walnuts, but that teacher wouldn't listen.

I never got the strap but my sister did and she could only been about six at the time. She was not paying attention, the teacher said, she was probably just daydreaming. I thought it was pretty cruel. Needless to remark they had to contend with my mother after *that* incident.

While we were living in Scotland the coronation of Queen Elizabeth the Second took place. We happily put a poster in our sitting room window facing the road saying 'God Save Queen Elizabeth the Second'. A brick was thrown through the glass. Of course she was Queen Elizabeth the First up there!

It was a glorious day for the celebration. Street parties were held and there was a fantastic costume parade for all the children. Mother made our costumes and we went as Peace, Progress and Prosperity. I don't remember exactly what we wore. I think I had a sort of Grecian dress, Hugo was in something like a spaceman's outfit and Jo had a fruit and food and money theme to her Prosperity costume. The maddening thing was that both she and Hugo won prizes but I did not.

I had also had to put up with mother's method of making my hair curly, something that caused me sleepless nights. After washing my hair she would roll my hair up in lengths of cotton rags, torn from old sheets. By the morning my hair would be dry, but the hard little bundles kept me awake half the night.

Another popular outing in the village was the cinema. All the kids went on a Saturday morning. It cost sixpence to sit in the first six rows on wooden benches. Our parents had to pay much more to sit at the back on plush seats!

One of the sad people in the village, befriended by my father, was a former hangman from one of the big prisons. The poor man used to have terrible nightmares of the times when he'd hanged prisoners. He would come and sit for hours in total depression talking to my parents. He said the only way he could sleep at night was to drink himself into oblivion. He was by this time totally against capital punishment believing it did not do any good and had a terrible effect on everyone else in the prison and all those connected with the prisoner being hung. The worst thing for him was that he wasn't sure he hadn't hung innocent men.

Daddy also became involved with an entrepreneur who had invented how to freeze dry vegetables. It was the very beginning of what was to become an enormous business. Unfortunately the man was not a very clever business man and the company folded.

Pocket Money

We had two ways of earning pocket money while living in Scotland. Every September we scoured the hedgerows and gardens for rosehips, which we collected, took into school where they were weighed and then sent off to the rosehip syrup factory. The more we collected the more money we made and so it was very competitive. My mother was very cross when she found one of the pupils in our back garden pinching the rosehips we had been eyeing up for our collection.

The other method was to go 'potato picking' in October when we had an especially long half term – three weeks. It was a very gruelling, back-breaking way of harvesting potatoes. Nowadays one tractor does it all, but back then a tractor would move along the furrows turning them over and exposing the potatoes, which we picked up by hand and put into baskets. I recall Hugo and me almost crawling home with aching backs, but the money was good!

The deaths of my grandparents

My grandmother died first and then only a few months later my grandfather followed her. I still remember my mother saying that my grandmother must have been in the front of the hearse with the driver at her own funeral. She loathed being driven slowly and as the hearse moved along the streets in a solemn fashion it gradually got faster and faster and by the time they reached the end of the town speed limit, it was travelling at about seventy miles per hour with all the procession of mourners tearing along after it. Actually my sister tells a different story about the hearse. Apparently my grandfather desperately needed to go to the loo and mother told the driver to speed up and pass the hearse so that they could stop at a hotel on the way, but every time they tried to pass, the hearse speeded up and the procession went faster and faster.

CHAPTER 6
BACK TO SUSSEX

Westfield

We became much better off when mother's part of the family trust was released and so we headed back to Sussex and a small village called Westfield, part way between Hastings and Rye. There we bought our first house, a delightful Queen Anne cottage with the wooden half boarding popular in Sussex and Kent.

The house had a smallish garden at the front and about half an acre at the back with lots of fruit trees in both. In the front one there was a big tree that was always covered with beautiful looking but disgustingly tasting apples. One day we left in the car to go into Hastings. Mother realised she had forgotten her handbag and we turned around only to find a couple of lads in the front garden scrumping the horrid apples. Instead of mother telling them off, she led them round to the back garden and pointed out the good fruit. They were so astonished they just took two each and left. They never came back again.

In one of the old trees we built a tree house. Another memory is of sitting underneath the tree with a big bowl of soup, and my rotten little brother deliberately pouring water down through the floorboards all over me and into my soup.

Hugo also set all the raspberry canes on fire in the same garden. I think he was running around with a burning rag on the end of a stick. Although we didn't get any raspberries that year, the following one they were fantastic!

Life improved as we were really settled for the first time in our lives.

All three of us children were enrolled in the local village school –

and we bought our first television! BBC 1 was the only channel and broadcasting, in black and white, began at six o'clock in the evening. This was all that was available in those days, but to our great excitement we were able to watch mother's book, 'The Blakes by Alison Wright', (her pseudonym and the name of her aunt). It had been adapted for children's television in five parts. It was loosely based on our life in the bus. Mother's book went on to be used as a teaching aid in schools all over the world.

My mother became a part time helper at Westfield village school and I clearly remember her coming home laughing after the first day of the new autumn term. A small boy, a farmer's son, came to school very proudly dressed in his new school uniform. He was in the infant class, and as it was the first day of school, he was given some paper and pencils and told to do a drawing. After lunch he was asked to do something equally unexciting. I think it was playing in the sand pit. He got up from his desk, walked out of the room and my mother, who followed him out, found him struggling into his coat and hat.

"Why are you putting on your coat?" she asked.

"I'm goin' 'ome!"

"But you can't go home yet, It isn't time," replied my mother.

"I'm goin' 'ome, because I'll never get a bloody scholarship in this place!" It was in the days of the eleven plus. He was just five years old!

Village Life

Life in Westfield was filled with activities. I joined the Girl Guides under the supervision of a fairly tough leader, Mrs Bather, while Hugo became a member of the Boy Scouts and mother directed numerous plays and shows.

So many memories come crowding in of those days. One of Hugo's Scout friends, who had a crush on me for a while, was a teenager called Keith Featherstone. I remember Keith well as on one occasion he arrived with his coat bulging. It was, he said, his poaching jacket and at that moment was filled with a brace of pheasants he'd nicked from a local estate. His mum loved pheasant he told us!

On another occasion mother befriended two spinster ladies who were very eccentric. They were kindly but odd. Mother came home one day laughing because one of their broody hens had abandoned its nest with a dozen or so semi-incubated eggs. As they didn't have an electric incubator one of the ladies retired to bed with the eggs and proceeded to stay there until the chicks hatched out ten days later!

When I was about eleven I became a Sunday school teacher at the village church and my brother joined the choir at about the same time. I lasted longer than Hugo. His first contretemps came when he decided - during a service, and right in the middle of the sermon - to throw sweets across the aisle to the choir boys on the other side. His next effort was to join the choir football team. He was duly elected captain – never quite sure why! Then, as soon as he was captain, he disbanded the entire team.

His final misdemeanour occurred when a visiting vicar was preaching. Our own vicar was hidden from the congregation by the buttress of the stone arch in the Norman Church. Hugo, who had a high pitched voice in those days, suddenly noticed that our vicar had dozed off, and was indeed snoring gently, said in a carrying voice that echoed round the church, announced to the assembled people he said, "Look at the vicar, he's gone to sleep!". The congregation burst into roars of laughter and Hugo was dismissed from the choir.

This story was bettered many years later when our local vicar in Cheshire told us about another vicar, who had just acquired a brand new clip-on microphone. During the service he really needed to visit the lavatory and so while the rather long psalm was droning out, he nipped into the vestry to perform. Unfortunately he forgot to switch off his microphone and the congregation was entertained by his expressions of satisfaction!

Jenny Bather

Hugo and I both passed the eleven plus and went to Rye Grammar School. I was a year ahead of him. Mrs Bather, the Guide Captain's middle daughter, Jenny, became my best friend. She was always in trouble – especially at home. On one occasion, being of an inquisitive nature, Jenny decided to take her father's barometer to bits to see how it worked. Not surprisingly she was unable to put it back together again. Stuffing the parts inside it, and with no attempt to screw the back on, she simply re-hung it. Later that day her father came along, tapped the glass on the front, only to find the entire works land at his feet. Jenny told her parents that Hugo had done it. Years later, not knowing what she'd said, I inadvertently mentioned the episode to her mother, only to get my foot heavily trodden upon by Jenny who was furious I'd let the secret out!

Starres
(See photograph)

The Queen Anne cottage we lived in was called 'Starres'. I believe it had been called that for centuries. It had a small front garden, but in the half an acre at the back we often had Guide or Scout meetings in the summer. The house itself was on three floors. My parents and I had bedrooms on the first floor, while Hugo and Jo were up in the attic. Downstairs there was the kitchen, a small drawing room, a dining room with black and white Marley tiles, and Daddy's study.

Whenever mother wanted the tiles polished in the dining room, she would put the polish on the floor and hand out old pairs of woollen socks to whomever of our school friends were there, and we would slide and skate around until the floor was lovely and shiny! It was easier and cheaper than buying an electric polisher.

When we moved into Starres we had very few books. Mother had lost many of her lovely leather bound books during a cooker fire we had in the bus. At this time my father was addicted to going to auction sales. He brought home all sorts of things until my mother finally stopped him from attending the regular bi-weekly sales. This was after the time he came back with a selection of fairly tatty, some even rusty, biscuit tins together with boxes and boxes of books. These were to fill up our almost empty shelves in his study. The only problem was that they had come from an old vicarage and were composed entirely

43

of matching hymn and Common Prayer books. He hadn't looked to see what gems he was buying. Mother wanted to throw them out immediately. Even our local church wasn't interested in taking any of them but Daddy insisted we kept them for a few years until we gradually weeded them out as we had enough books to fill the shelves.

It was in this study that my father had one of his many clairvoyant experiences. A lady came to visit us and my father immediately asked who she'd brought with her. He described a young man in an old fashioned uniform and suggested that when she got home she looked through old family photographs. Sure enough she discovered who he was. He had been killed in the First World War.

Acting

Among the plays mother produced were the fairy scenes from 'A Midsummer Night's Dream'; and 'Toad of Toad Hall'. In 'A Midsummer Night's Dream' I played the part of Titania, Jenny was Puck and my father played the part of Bottom. The play was performed in our garden among the apple trees – it was magical. By the time we got to 'Toad' I was assistant stage manager and Jenny was an unbelievably good Toad. But she was a nightmare to direct as you never knew what she would do next. I remember her bringing the house down while she lay on a couch heaving her stomach up and down, quite ruining one of Ratty's speeches.

It was while I was at Rye Grammar School that I took part in both prose and verse competitions at school and also in the Hastings Musical Festival. Although very shy, mother's intensive coaching made sure I won almost all the competitions at school and several in the festival. It was very good training for the classes, lectures and talks I have been doing later in my life and I am eternally grateful to my mother for encouraging me (*forcing* me as one of my granddaughters said of me when I persuaded her to continue with her golf!), to take part.

A group of us attended a local dance evening in Rye one evening. I can't have been more than fifteen. It wasn't obvious to begin with but a young man seemed to be interested in me and asked me to dance, much to the rage and fury of his girlfriend. I hadn't realised they were an item. This girl was making horrid remarks, and so to get my own back I persuaded my friends to point at her feet and laugh. This is very uncomfortable thing to do to anyone because they have no idea what is wrong. At the end of the dance we all left. She was waiting outside for me and hit me as I walked through the door. I'm afraid I hit her back and accidentally knocked her earring off. She became angrier and angrier, demanding that I pick it up. I just told her that I didn't touch Woolworth's things and so would not pick it up. Fortunately her boyfriend pulled her off. Nowadays, she probably would have knifed me.

My First Boyfriends

I remember my first real boyfriend. His name was Keith Baker and he took me to the cinema. We went on the bus and he bought me a box of 'Black Magic' chocolates with the money his mother had given to him for just such an event. The romance didn't last long though and my next boyfriend was Peter Stretton. After we broke up several months later, he tempted me to go out with him again by bringing a 'four legged baby chick' in a bottle to school to show me! Mother dined out on this for ages.

The next, non-boyfriend, I had, was a young man, named Colin Pugh, who was about two years ahead in school. He used to buy bags of cherries for me which I refused to eat. Jenny became very cross when I repulsed his offerings as she wanted them. He also wrote poetry for me. One of the poems began, 'Your pensive moonlight face'. I threw them all out but mother was furious because she said she could have stuck them on the walls of the downstairs loo, which was in need of decorating. She said it would have been very entertaining to sit there and read his letters and verses.

Hugo also enraged my parents when he systematically pinched photographs of me to sell to several of the boys. It was only when my mother caught him removing a portrait from a photo frame that she found out what he was up to. "I can get ten bob for this!" he argued when my mother made him put it back.

Daddy's past life

It must have been during this time that one of my father's sons from his first marriage arrived to 'look him up'. It was years later that my Aunt Natalie told us about the visit because at the time we were unaware of who the man was. Daddy always denied he was actually his son. It may have been this that caused my parents to go off to the local Registry Office to legalise their relationship. At the time none of us knew anything about it. I believe my brother was told, but I didn't find out until I was about twenty-two or three that we had all been born 'out of wedlock'. It was to cause a great deal of problems many years later when we contested the Family Trust – which we lost. Scottish Law being different from English in that the moment my parents got married we became legitimate in England but not in Scotland.

Rye Grammar School

Rye Grammar School was a wonderful institution. There were only about three hundred and fifty children there – quite small by today's standards of modern comprehensive schools.

I enjoyed most of it although I hated the Latin classes, especially double Latin first thing on a Thursday morning. Mr Silver, our Latin teacher was extremely attractive, but poor man, every time he suggested I was more suited to studying Home Economics, mother thrust me back into his classes saying that at a Grammar School I should be studying the Classics. I remember his comment in one of Hugo's progress reports, it simply said: 'Hugo has not mastered the more sophisticated art of thinking silently.' In the same year his art teacher simply said, 'Talkative!' Both correct I suspect.

My School Uniform

On the whole I was happy at school but do not have the brain my mother and brother had. They were 'off the clock' as several of the next generations also are. However my English teacher, Mr Derby, was always giving me extra credit marks – I always thought it was a bit odd. He did have a habit of teasing me about my school cardigans. Looking back I am not really surprised. Mother used to knit them for me. They were *awful!* For one thing, she couldn't knit very well and secondly she would get bored with knitting the same design. I had one cardigan that had at least a dozen different patterns – none of which matched, on the front alone. Fortunately she at least stuck to the right colour, which was a fairly boring brown.

My school hats were, if anything, worse! All the other girls had new hats bought for them by their caring mothers. Not that mother didn't care, she did, but she did not see why she should go and buy me a new hat when she could raid the acting box and pull out brown felt hats that had been abandoned by my great aunt Hilda. She did have to unpick the designer pleats and, on one occasion, remove a small bunch of feathers attached to the side! No wonder the boys on the bus threw my hats out of the window! To this day I can see myself climbing on to the school bus dressed in a squashed school hat, (I scrunched it up to try and disguise its antiquity), a blue checked gingham dress with one lapel failing to lie flat, (she'd struggled with it), a strange hand-knitted cardigan with one sleeve slightly longer than the other and the only official clothing hidden under my skirt – dark brown elasticised knickers. Passion killers the boys called them. Even she couldn't copy these!

Other teachers who live on in my memory are, the maths teacher, poor man he never did get me to understand anything other than simple mental arithmetic. I recall him hitting me across the back of my hand with a ruler when I was messing about with my geometry.

Then there was Miss Lumb, a wonderful history teacher, who, I believe, had been at the opening of the Tutenkamum pyramid. She really knew her subject, but did have a problem, a lisp, and so we all fought *not* to sit in the front row as you were likely to get a shower when she talked.

The Headmaster who taught scripture, known as divinity, probably guessed that my homework was done by my mother. There was also

47

Miss Dann, who taught French. She always wore very masculine tweed suits with a man's tie. Looking back she was probably a lesbian, but in those days I had never heard anything about that sort of thing.

I played hockey, netball and rounders for the school, but hated gymnastics and was not very keen on the field sports such as the high jump.

I also played in the village 'stoolball' team, which was a strange game that only seemed to be played in Sussex. It was sort of a game of cricket played in the air. Batsmen had round wooden bats which were held in front of a wooden board about a forty centimetres square, attached to a shoulder high wooden pole. There were two of these with a batsman in front of each. I can't remember how far apart they were. A hard ball, smaller than a cricket ball, was used and the aim of the bowler was to hit the board. 'Runs' were scored by the batsman running between the boards.

Although I didn't realise it at the time, I was badly teased at school by a couple of girls in my year. At the time it was teasing, bordering on bullying. I thought later that it might have been because I had boyfriends before they had and perhaps they were jealous, whatever it was I often used to go home in tears, feeling miserable.

However it could have been more serious with another girl who was very aggressive. She decided to try and thump me, as she had done with several other girls, but I stood up to her and we became the best of friends. Helga Starnes, for that was her name, was German. Her father had been killed in the War by the Allies and her mother later met an Englishman and married him. He was a local Sussex farmer. I will always remember the time I went to visit her for the day and her mother told us to go and kill a chicken. Poor old Helga tried to wring its neck and failed, so she got a chopper out and cut its head off!

Helga's father bred Red Poll cattle for milking while Helga was gradually building up a small herd of Jerseys. Sometimes, when it was market day, Helga would ride in the back of the cattle truck with the cattle. She wore leather lederhosen underneath her gymslip and on an occasion, when she smelt particularly bad from the cattle, the Latin master threw her out of the classroom!

One classic day, during the scripture lesson, which was taught by a very nice, but very short sighted little man, Helga, who usually spent her time tearing the back pages off the Bible he'd given her, crawled up the aisle between the desks to where I was sitting.

"Anna," she whispered, "My best cow calved last night and I called her Anna after you." No greater compliment could have been given than to be called after one of Helga's beautiful little cows!

Looking back now I do think she must have had a very hard time. It was only a matter of a few years after the War and she was very Germanic having come from Berlin.

It was while living in Westfield that I became totally disturbed by fox-hunting. The local hunt was meeting at the pub opposite the front of our house. Hugo and I decided to follow on foot. Mother tried to dissuade me. My grandmother had been mad on fox hunting and so we insisted. Unfortunately Hugo and I were there 'for the kill'. There were some young riders out for the first time. The whipper-in grabbed the live fox and cut off its tail – this was to brush blood over the faces of these children, and then he threw the squealing animal into the pack of hounds. Mercifully for the poor creature it was torn to shreds in seconds, but it is an image I have never forgotten.

Our French Pen-friends

It was while we were living in Westfield that both Hugo and I acquired French pen friends. Michele Colomb was my friend and Hugo's was Gepe Proy, (pronounced Jaypee Proir). They were both only children. Gepe's mother adopted him at the end of the war. We always thought she looked like a 'water boatman' as she moved around, darting from one place to the next. She was very short sighted and wore spectacles with extra thick lenses. She never married, but during the war she had been very brave as the leader of the Resistance in the Le Puy-en-Velez area of France. During one holiday in Le Puy, we watched her as she dashed backwards and forwards across the street in and out of shops! I believe Gepe became a dentist and lives in Lyon now.

Michele's parents were lovely. Madame Colomb was the typical

French woman, always looking very chic. I think Michele found her quite difficult but adored her father. I understand that her mother gave herself airs and graces, although she came from a much more working class family, while M. Colomb's family were aristocratic. The reverse of ours. Monsieur Colomb used to tease us. On one occasion when visiting us in England, M. Colomb, who was driving a Renault car covered with Prunelle advertising, was encouraged by my brother,

"Go faster M. Colomb, go faster!" and he did, quite terrifying a learner driver, who had the disadvantage of being up in front of him on the narrow lanes in Sussex. Both he and Hugo laughed outrageously.

M. Colomb's family owned one of the local distilleries where they made the delicious Prunelle du Velez. Mother was always delighted to receive bottles of it when they came to visit us in England.

Monsieur and Madame Colomb are both dead at the time of writing. However, although I lost touch with Michele for many years, we have made contact again, years and years after I left home, in fact I was probably about forty-three when we again met up. Michael and I managed to find their new address and talk to the Colomb's before going to visit them. By this time they had retired and moved to Craponne sur Arzon in the Auvergne.

They entertained us to a magnificent meal in the house which had been in M. Colomb's family for centuries. We were amazed to find they had four original Aubusson tapestries hanging on their walls. When I mentioned them, Madame Colomb just shrugged her shoulders and said they'd always been there since they were new.

Before we sat down for dinner, the Colomb's entertained us with some old cine films, which they had taken when we were teenagers. It was a riot watching Hugo!

The food was delicious, but the wine better. Monsieur Colomb had been down into his cellar and brought up two bottles of Givret Chamberton which had lain there for forty five years! He opened one of them, which fortunately was perfect, and left it to breathe for six hours. It was followed by some wonderful champagne.

Over the meal, we naturally enquired about Michele. Their story of her life in Paris with her completely mental husband really shocked us. Michele had been living in Paris for ten or so years to a man she knew from Le Puy days. While in Paris he became obsessed with cleanliness. Towards the end he was forcing poor Michele to wash her hands for at least twenty minutes non stop. When they went shopping, which was rare, he wouldn't buy anything that was on the bottom shelf of the supermarket and so sometimes they went from one shop to another. Michele was never allowed to go out by herself, or to send or take telephone calls and he only allowed them to have ten meals or less a *week!* Often she was deprived of sleep for days at a time. She was trapped both mentally and physically. Monsieur and Madame Colomb were naturally distraught and did not know what to do as they were not allowed any contact with her or she with them.

I told them about Dame Felicitas, who came into our lives when Jo was about twenty-one. (More about her later, but she seemed to be able to perform miracles through prayer.) I said I would write to Dame Felicitas upon our arrival back in England, which I did. The strangest thing happened. Within two weeks, Michele and her husband were told that the water in their apartment had to be cut off every day, all day, for six weeks. For someone who insisted that every plate had to be washed at least six times this was absolutely appalling! They moved to Craponne where they used an apartment immediately below Michele's parents, who were forced to listen to Michele's distress until one day they called the police who came and carted the husband off. When Monsieur and Madame Colomb entered the apartment they found *everything* swathed or covered in blue plastic!

On our next trip Michele and I met up again for the first time in nearly thirty years and her parents treated us like royalty. We sent Madame Colomb a big bouquet of flowers when we left and the sight of it encouraged Michele to begin painting again. She has had numerous exhibitions since.

We are Moving again!

We were very happy at Rye, but sadly a year before I took my 'O' levels and after Jo sat her eleven plus – but before her results came through, my parents decided to move again, this time to Eastbourne.

The shock of going from a small co-ed grammar school to a large all girls' high school at the age of fifteen and a half was devastating and I hated it. Jo was told she had failed the eleven plus and subsequently went to Ravenscroft, a private girl's school in Eastbourne. We always teased Jo because when she left Ravenscroft, it closed down and later, the same thing happened when she went to a finishing school in Switzerland, Les Volets Jaunes, suffered a similar demise!

We were never sure why we moved again, but maybe it was because people heard rumours about my parent's previous relationship, and certainly back in the early fifties it would have been frowned upon.

CHAPTER 7
EASTBOURNE

The Sailing Club

Soon after arriving in Eastbourne, my brother began nagging my parents to join the Eastbourne Sailing Club. When Hugo started he didn't stop until he got his own way. It was really Hugo who was keen, but we all became members because it was cheaper to join as a family.

Hugo was fourteen and I was fifteen and a half at the time. It wasn't long before Hugo had nagged our parents into buying him a boat. He got a Graduate; a twelve foot long wooden sailing dinghy. Mother had a brilliant idea for a name for his boat. She wanted to call the boat 'banjo' – a *little* 'b' for Hugo, 'an' for Anna, 'jo' for Jo. 'My brother was furious, but we all thought it was an excellent idea!

My brother was very outgoing and talked to everyone, while I was content to sit quietly on the pebbles which covered the entire beach, just watching the hustle and rush of the sailors preparing their dinghies for the afternoon race.

It wasn't long before we both became obsessed with sailing and I will always remember my first sail. A young man, Martin Bedford, he was probably only sixteen, asked me if I would like to crew for him in his Graduate. I hadn't a clue!

"I've never sailed before."

"That's OK, I'll teach you", he said, pulling me to my feet. I can remember stumbling nervously down the beach, dislodging hard granite pebbles. We got nearer and nearer to the waves rolling in and splashing the bow of boat, waiting to be launched through the surf breaking further out and blocking our way to the calmer water beyond.

I gingerly climbed in while Martin held it steady and told me to hang on to the jib sheet. The smell of the sea was strong now, sharp and cold and I sat huddled trying to take in what Martin was telling me as we headed towards the starting line and the sound of the starting gun. We didn't win that day. However, he asked me to crew for him again.

My first capsize

Several trips later, and by this time I really loved sailing, we were racing out towards the windward buoy. The little boat was charging along on a broad reach, with sails billowing out. Feet firmly tucked under the foot straps, I leant out as far as possible to keep the dinghy upright, causing waves to run along the sides of the dinghy. I laughed with the sheer exhilaration of controlling and guiding this small boat, racing alongside other boats. I clearly remember turning towards Martin, grinning my head off – but he wasn't there! All I could see were the soles of his feet disappearing through the spume of the bow wave. He hadn't put his feet under his feet straps and he had been washed overboard.

I just sat there wondering what to do. The boat was completely out of control. The mainsail flapped madly and then, in slow motion, it gently capsized and I was catapulted into the freezing grey sea of the English Channel. Gasping, I hung on to the side of the dinghy and waited for Martin to swim up. Together we righted it, climbed in and set off again in pursuit of the other boats. No going in to change into dry clothes – sailors who race have to be hardy souls.

He and I went on to win many events, including the Junior Graduate Championships, which took place that year at Southend-on-Sea. Out of four races we came in first *four* times! Martin was an excellent helmsman and over the years I became a very good crew.

During my years at the Eastbourne Sailing Club I sailed Graduates, a Firefly, Enterprises, a National 12, an International 14, a Merlin Rocket, and a '505'. The Merlin was owned by Derek Farrant, a cousin of Jenny Bather's future husband, Roger Farrant. I was sixteen at the time he invited me out to dinner. I remember wearing a dark blue cotton dress with a small, real flower, corsage. Derek was twenty-nine and had recently broken up after a long relationship. I never told him, but it was his boat, his Austin Healey and, that he was the British national champion of the Merlin Rocket class which really attracted me! The relationship foundered when his mother, who knew my mother, told him how young I was. I think one of my most poignant memories of Derek was towing the Merlin behind the Austin Healey along the straight road between Pevensey Bay and Eastbourne at probably more than eighty miles an hour. Completely mad, but great fun.

Then Ian Barron came into my life! I became his crew and, for more years than I care to remember, and although he wasn't, I thought he was totally wonderful. Ian owned a National 12; I can still remember its number – 1444. Ian had named it Consternation, commonly known as 'Constipation'.

Ian was an absolute blighter. I was the best crew he ever had and we did very well in all competitions but what really upset me was that he would invite gorgeous models down from London, allow me to prepare the boat for sailing, and then come rushing down the beach at the very last moment to go out for the race. Ian was also useless in his time-keeping. Many a time he was late and I had to stand in the shallows of the water, holding the boat, ready for Ian just to jump into, because you were not allowed any help after the 'ten minute' gun was fired, and off we would go, dashing to the start line for the beginning of the race!

He also said he couldn't afford to buy any jamming cleats to hold the jib sheets. I was expected to hang on whatever the weather. I remember on one occasion, when it had been blowing particularly hard, my hands became blistered during the Saturday afternoon race. I arrived on Sunday morning with plasters over the blisters. As usual we were late and shot off towards the start line only to find that Ian had forgotten the bungs! Frantically looking round for something to stuff into the bung holes to stop the water pouring in, Ian noticed my plasters. He made me take them off and stuffed them in the holes. My blisters turned to open wounds as I grimly hung on to the jib sheets. Salt water and wet ropes do not mix well with open blisters. After the race I opened my palms and said, "Look at my hands they're bleeding."

Ian replied, "And look at my jib sheets, they were new on today and you've covered them with blood – don't ever do that again!" And he wasn't joking. However we have laughed about it many a time since then.

I almost always crewed for Ian when racing, but would sometimes go off to sail just for fun. On one memorable occasion I went out for a sail with Nicholas Bruford, known as Cocky Bruford. Nick owned a Firefly. We decided to sail down towards Beachy Head as it was quite windy and we took advantage of planing (surfing) on a broad reach. When we were near to the cliffs we really raced in towards the foot of them. It was great fun and it was only when we turned to sail back to the Club that we realised it was going to be very hard work tacking backwards and forwards against the wind for some considerable distance. We did think about sailing on down to Seaford but thought we ought to go back as we didn't think either of our parents would be pleased to drive there to fetch us and the boat back. We arrived to find quite a contingent of people. My mother was there together with Nick's father, (who was also the Club Commodore), and the head of the lifeboat crew were lined up waiting for us. They had actually pulled the lifeboat out ready to launch and come to our rescue when they saw us rounding the pier. We got a severe ticking off. My brother, who was with my mother, had, with great presence of mind, grabbed the lifeboat box off the wall of the Clubhouse and gone along the rows of tourists who were watching the whole proceedings and persuaded them to fill the box.

Teenage Ball

Each year my grandmother's friend Mrs Humphries-Davis would organise a 'Teenage Ball' at the Grand Hotel. The idea was to get us used to going to social events like balls. It was run on very much the lines of debutante events – except that we were all younger than the average deb, the average age was about fifteen.

Invitations were sent out and we duly turned up in all our finery. Mrs H.D. and several contemporaries of hers sat round in chairs to make sure nobody was left out, and 'woe betide' any young man who attempted to dance with the same girl twice! It was good in a way as no girl was left sitting as a 'wallflower'. Those formidable ladies made sure of that!

Mother's Cooking

My mother was one of those lovely people who really enjoyed seeing people. She always said that if someone came to visit then you stopped everything you were doing, especially if it was house-work, because that was always there but the people were not. She was a shocking cook, having never learnt. My grandmother did not believe in her daughters doing anything practical, she could also afford servants! Mother used to *count* heads and feed whoever was there, with some disastrous results. On one occasion she lost me a boyfriend! It was an evening when several people did turn up unexpectedly. We were having a beef stew for supper and there wasn't enough to go round. It was in the days of the little *lion* eggs. The advertisers were encouraging everybody to 'add an egg'. She did. Twelve of them. She broke them straight into the top of the boiling stew. It looked awful with the yolks turning a rather nasty shade of khaki and the white breaking up in little globules. My boyfriend took one look and suddenly remembered he was supposed to be home for supper. I never saw him again.

On another occasion when we had friends to dinner, mother made a lime flavoured jelly with *milk*. She had over ordered from the milkman and also, she thought it would be more nutritious. She presented the rabbit shaped jelly to us and at that moment the electricity went off. The whole room was completely dark except for the jelly which sat in the middle of table glowing like a phosphorescent evil monster. We refused to eat it after that.

Mother was very generous with her time helping other people; she did more of that than housekeeping! One Christmas she volunteered to make the Christmas puddings for the large senior citizens club. It was decided they would need seventeen puds. Mother duly mixed them; filled pudding bowls and topped them with greaseproof paper and squares of an old bed sheet, washed of course, and smothered dry flour into the pieces of fabric. Then she thought about how the heck she was going to cook them. Suddenly a brilliant idea came into her mind! She remembered the occasion when she had turned on the water heater on her washing machine and forgotten to switch it off again and the water became so hot it actually boiled. Mother decided to clean out the machine and pack the puddings into it. It worked! The puddings boiled beautifully, except that seventeen had gone in and only sixteen came out!

To this day I can hear her say, "What if I've broken the machine and have to call the man out? What do I tell him? Do I say that it is one of your father's socks that stuck in the motor, or do I admit that it is Christmas pudding?" Fortunately she didn't have to get the man out.

Years later Ian Barron, who adored my eccentric mother, said that she kept the house in such a mess that often the only way to get in was to climb in through the window! I know I used to sometimes come home at the time my father had specified and then climb back out through the window again. Poor man, I knew he would lie awake worrying, and because of his ill heath I didn't like to argue about the early hours he restricted us to. I hasten to add that this only happened after I had been living away at college when nobody oversaw what time I came in and so it was difficult to suddenly be told to be back in by 10 o'clock.

One of my first jobs was as a junior receptionist at the Cavendish Hotel on the sea front in Eastbourne. At that time it was a five star hotel and ranked alongside the Grand as one of the two best hotels in the area. The other junior receptionist was a very nicely brought up young woman called Barbara Lockett. As an only child she was not used to the sort of family we were. Mother invited Barbara to supper one evening and, as often happened, Mother and Hugo got into a discussion that rapidly became quite virulent. Hugo lost his temper, picked up his cup of tea and threw it all over mother. She, without pausing to draw breath, grabbed the teapot, took off the lid and tipped the entire contents straight over my brother's head. There was a stunned silence, before, simultaneously Barbara began to say that

Hugo was awful for being so rude to his mother, and Hugo and mother burst into uncontrollable laughter. Barbara left shortly afterwards and never came again to visit us.

Then there was poor John Sogno. He was quite a few years older than me was but he would keep coming round and asking me out. He was not a very attractive man and Hugo and I called him John 'Soggy-nose'! I have always felt very bad about our behaviour because he was a very nice man and did not deserve our unkindness.

Old Family Linen

It was while we were living in Eastbourne that Mother found the old linen. She had washed various bits of napkins and towels and held one of the pieces up to the light to see if it was really clean. Looking at it carefully she realised that there was a date woven into the fabric – 1707, along with two names, the names are James Davies (the J more like a modern I), and Mary Haigs. It appears that this piece may have been made as part of the trousseau as the 'A's are in the shape of hearts with flowers etc woven in.

The other two pieces are dated 1717. Same names but with the hearts and flowers replaced by hunting scenes. We think Mary must have married him by then and the romantic period had worn off!

The Victoria and Albert Museum in London have one piece hanging in the British (or English) Gallery. It is dated 1708 and belonged to the Earl of Hopetoun.

The linen was certainly Scottish because in Scotland you could have your own designs made in those days. You didn't have to be an aristocrat; however you would have had to be wealthy because it would have been very expensive.

Glyndebourne

With mother's interest in the theatre, I became involved with a small group of teenagers, including the head boy of Eastbourne Grammar

School. We decided to enter a youth one act play competition. The play we chose was totally obscure. Written by T.S. Eliot, it was called 'A Fragment of an Agon' and I never understood what it was about until the final performance. We sailed through the preliminary rounds to reach the final which was held on the huge stage at Glyndebourne. What an experience that was and the lighting engineers were amazing. We told them we wanted the impression of our little rubber tree to grow on the backcloth, while the shadow of a noose dropped on to the same white cloth. I played the part of Snow and I think another character was named Sweeney. We won the competition by miles.

Soon after this I took my 'O' levels, of which I passed five out of six and, immediately after the last exam, I left school and took up a full time job at the Cavendish for about eight months before going off to Edinburgh. The one I failed was Maths. I was interviewed by the maths teacher at Eastbourne High School a few months before I took the exam. Our conversation went something like this.

"I don't understand why sometimes you write out the equation in a very odd way, but get the right answer and on other occasions, you write down the correct method but get the answer completely wrong."

I responded with, "That's easy. When I get the answer right and the method wrong, it is because my younger brother has worked it out for me but doesn't know how to write it out. When I get the answer *wrong* it is because I add, subtract, multiply or divide by the first number that comes into my head!"

She just looked stunned as she nodded and said, "Yes, that would explain it." She gave up trying to help me after that.

High School Friend.

Hugo followed me out of school a couple of years later. It was such a shame because he had a very good brain but he insisted he couldn't stay on at school after the behaviour of a friend of his called Keith who, aged sixteen, was going out with a very naïve fifteen year old. Her parents were equally naïve and were totally shattered when they discovered she was pregnant. Keith at first denied his responsibility and then boasted about it. It was too much for Hugo who was very keen on her, as all the boys were. She was such a pretty girl, the spitting image of a young Brigitte Bardot. My brother became so angry that he walked into his Headmaster's office and told him he was leaving school, which he did the same day, leaving mother with the quandary of what to do with him.

Her parents were all for packing her off to a home where she could stay until the baby arrived some five months later. Mother stepped in and invited her to come and stay at our house until much nearer the birth. (I thought later, after I knew our history and the fact that mother became pregnant before being married, although she was in her thirties and not sixteen, she must have realised what it was like and been very sympathetic.) In that way she could continue to do school work at home. Although very young in mind, she also had an excellent brain and planned to go on to university, which she eventually did when she was offered a place at Cambridge. It was extraordinary that nobody in the town found out she was still living in Eastbourne, except our family doctor of course, and one of my boyfriends who later dated her for quite a long time. After the baby arrived, she returned to school, not in Eastbourne but at Rye where mother had managed to get her a place.

The Cavendish Hotel

I loved working at the Cavendish and have many happy memories, one of which was when I won half-a-crown from John Betjeman, who was then the Poet Laureate. He had come down to stay at the hotel along with several other celebrities involved in a radio show. I was asked to show Mr Betjeman to his room on the fourth floor. We ascended in the old fashioned open lift with wrought iron bars and a pageboy dressed in a burgundy suit and small round hat. Upon leaving the room, which he said was fine, we made our way back to the lift. Mr Betjeman then asked me if I was going down in it instead of walking. I said yes. He then challenged me that if I reached the ground floor by lift before he could run down the staircase, which circled the lift shaft, he'd give me half-a-crown. I bribed the page with sixpence not to stop at any of the floors on the way down. We watched Mr Betjeman race down the stairs which circled the lift shaft and arrived at the same moment as Mr Betjeman, who was still dressed in his big floppy hat and long cloak flying out behind him, shouted, "You've won, you've won!" I catapulted straight into the arms of the manager who gave me a critical look but said nothing.

On another occasion I came home laughing. The auditors were in the hotel going through the books with a fine toothcomb. The book keeper, a fairly revolting little man, had been systematically stealing money for years. These auditors were attractive young men who had come down from London and they were perpetually teasing Barbara and me. One afternoon the phone at the front desk rang and the head receptionist, Margaret Connelly, answered it. She thought she was talking to one of the young men because a fairly high pitched voice said, "I want a room for thirty little men."

Margaret replied, "We only have one very small room with six very large beds in it."

It was not the auditors at all; it was the Thai Embassy in London who really wanted single, (little!) rooms for thirty of their staff! Margaret couldn't stop laughing and had to hand the phone over to someone else to make the reservations.

We, at the Cavendish thought we were superior to the Grand Hotel, our rival five star hotel, and certainly my grandmother refused to ever set foot inside the Grand after she'd walked past the back of it years before.

My Sister Jo

My sister Jo was always pinching my clothes and once, when mother and I were in Eastbourne shopping for my departure to Edinburgh, she suddenly said, "Look at that girl over there, what mother could have allowed her daughter to go out dressed like that!" It was *Jo* and so mother and I hurriedly crossed the street and pretended we, and we hoped, any of mother's friends, hadn't seen her.

Poor Jo was always jealous of me. I had many friends, but then

I was involved in so many things and all Jo wanted to do was to sit around in coffee bars. Once, when she was complaining about being bored, my father sat down and wrote a list of about thirty different activities and sports that Jo could join in with. She glanced down the list and said, "I don't want to do any of those things, I am so bored." At that point my father gave up the struggle.

Coffee Bars in Eastbourne

During my time in Eastbourne coffee bars and 'frothy coffee' were all the rage. The first one I went to was the Continental somewhere along the main street. Whenever I hear the song 'Volare' it takes me right back there. I mostly went there on Saturday morning before going on down to the sailing club. I used to sit there hoping that Ian Barron would come in, and then would be too shy to speak to him.

Later another coffee bar opened and was called 'ffinch's'. I had a summer job there and later Jo followed me. It was on two floors, ground floor a normal coffee bar, but the cellar area was a dark, and when the lights were full on, very dingy.

Cousin to the Queen

A young man I became acquainted with was a young guard's officer and who was, he said, a cousin to the Queen. One evening when he was staying in Eastbourne, he invited me out. At the time my father's health was deteriorating and he hardly left the big music room where we kept the television. Daddy used to watch it in the dark with all the curtains closed. When the young officer (I've forgotten his name) came to collect me, he had come straight from a regimental function and arrived still wearing his 'blues' dress uniform. Peering at him out of the gloom, my father suddenly said, "Why is my daughter going out with a bus conductor? And what's more – he's coloured!" The young man overheard the remark and dined out on it for years!

Other friends of Hugo's were Lady Anthea Lowry-Corrie and

Serena, (again I cannot recall her surname). Later, after Anthea married an Irish Earl, Jo and mother went over to stay with them. Driving from the airport my sister casually announced she hadn't seen a mad Irishman yet.

"Don't worry," replied Anthea's husband, "you will." Then a few miles further on, miles from anywhere, they passed an old man standing by the side of the road practising golf shots with his walking stick and stones from the verges. Jo and mother later pondered about whether it was a put up job or whether he was real.

But long before this happened I went off to Edinburgh to stay with my extremely batty Aunt Nathalie and to attend the Edinburgh College of Domestic Science fondly known as Athol Crescent or the Dough School.

CHAPTER 8
HUGO – 29th February 1944 – October 1995

Hugo's Life from 1960 onwards

After the Louise episode, Hugo decided to go to London to become an articled clerk in a large accountancy firm.

I recall the day he and Mother went to London to find him a flat. They travelled up by train. My father, who hadn't driven a car for some time, because he hadn't been well, offered to go with them to the station and drive the car home again. Mother stopped the car immediately behind a parked police car and jokingly told Daddy not to drive into it. As she and Hugo disappeared into the booking hall, my father did exactly what he'd been told not to do and crashed straight into the back of the car, much to the total astonishment of the two policemen sitting inside! Poor Daddy, he never drove again!

It was the same car my father crashed into the back of the police vehicle, that Mother a few months later took into Eastbourne to go shopping, forgot that she'd taken it, rode home on the bus complaining about the weight of the groceries and then reported to the police it had been stolen from the front of the house! They found it fairly quickly and greatly embarrassed she had to apologise.

Hugo and His Girlfriends

On one of my holidays from Edinburgh I went to ffinch's coffee bar (which Gavin Hogge managed several years later). Striking up a conversation with a girl who knew my brother she said that I must be

Hugo's younger sister. I denied it and replied that I was actually Hugo's *older* sister.

"Well how old are you?" was the curious question.

"I'm seventeen."

"You must be younger than Hugo because he's nineteen."

"No, you've got it wrong. My brother is a year and a half younger than I am."

At first she wouldn't believe me because my brother had shot such a line to dozens of girls from the various colleges and finishing schools. He'd told them he was at Oxford University but had been 'sent down' for some reason or other. As a student, he said, he didn't have any money and so the girls took pity on him and invited him, at their expense, to accompany them to dances and other events. They even came to collect him in their fancy cars! Needless to say my brother was very angry with me for letting it out he wasn't nineteen but was still only sixteen and attending the local Grammar School.

One day when Hugo was twenty-one he, Jo and Gavin Hogge walked into ffinch's Coffee Bar where Vicky Wessel was sitting with some of her friends from Rannies, (Rannies being the casual name for the Eastbourne cookery school). He took one look at Vicky, turned to Gavin and Jo and told them he'd just seen the girl he was going to marry. He then phoned Ian Barron, to ask him to immediately come down to ffinch's to meet Vicky – telling him he'd met the girl he was going to marry. Ian arrived to find a very quiet young woman, nothing like my brother's usual type.

When Hugo met Vicky, who was eighteen at the time, he had just started work at Oakdens and drove an old red Wolsley car that had been adapted for a disabled person. It had a large sign on the back – 'No Hand Signals', which always caused comments and definitely vulgar remarks!

I will say here that over the years all our sympathies have gone to Vicky. Hugo with his brilliant brain, his wit and enthusiasm was sometimes very difficult to live with. From time to time he did suffer from mood swings but he could be enormous fun and everybody thought the world of him. In later years when he, mother and his two sons, Robert and Ben got together they kept us all laughing so hard that we would almost be crying.

He thoroughly enjoyed his time in London as an articled clerk, not that he did a lot of work – but on the strength of having a dinner jacket and a white tie and tails he was invited to lots of the debutante parties given during the season. In this he was ably abetted by Gavin Hogge who became a lifelong friend. I think Gavin was much more interested in playing backgammon than earning money as an accountant!

Gavin Hogge's Description of Meeting Hugo

(Gavin became one of Hugo's best friends and he kindly wrote the following for me to include in the book. It is in the first person because I am using Gavin's words.)

I first met Hugo in April or May 1961 when I joined Allen, Baldry, Holman and Best (chartered accountants) in the City where we were both articled clerks. Hugo had started work there a month or two before I did.

He asked me if I needed a place to live as his mother had found him a flat in Mount Carmel Chambers (flat number 20), Dukes Lane, off Church Street, Kensington. So I moved in with Hugo, Mark Steele and Sebastian Thewes. At the time we joked that the flats were like an institution with green and cream paint everywhere. I went back recently to show Ginnie, (Gavin's wife) what a dump we had lived in, but it had been transformed into luxurious apartments with thick pile carpets, a lift and a doorman. I think when we were there the rent for the whole flat was £7 per week.

Having done no studies whatsoever, we both left Allen Baldry before any exams loomed in the spring of 1963 and went down to stay with Hugo's mother in Enys Road, Eastbourne. Hugo got a job for the summer, selling ice creams in Bournemouth, and I started work at ffinch's coffee bar in Grove Street, Eastbourne. The story goes that Hugo managed to decapitate his ice cream van under a low bridge, so I don't know how long that job lasted! He was certainly back in Eastbourne helping me in ffinch's where I was now manager through the winter of 1963/64.

I left Eastbourne in July 1964 and think Hugo got a job at Oakden & Co., Estate Agents in Cornfield Road, Eastbourne shortly afterwards. He enjoyed it so much that he persuaded me to join the profession and I started work at A.C. Draycott & Partners in the summer of 1965.

I was best man at his wedding to Vicky in June 1966 and Hugo was best man a month later when I married Ginnie.

Hugo, Marriage and Children

I remember Hugo's wedding which took place in Leicester on June 18th 1966. The day before the wedding the weather was foul and Mother got a terrible shock when she heard the news of the dreadful car crash which involved Uncle Hugo, his wife Ruth and their friends the Earl and Countess of Mar, who were all travelling together from Scotland. Ruth sadly died and the others were kept in hospital for several weeks. Hugo and Vicky looked, and were, very young on the day but Vicky proved to be an excellent wife and mother.

They lived in Bodle Street, Sussex before moving to Whatlington near Battle where they bought a lovely old house called Ringletts. They stayed there for ten years before moving into Eastbourne where they remained for a further eleven.

I think one of their mistakes was to convert an out building or old barn into a cottage for Mother to live in. Mother was one of those people whom everybody else seemed to get on well with but I certainly found her impossible to live with, as I suspect Vicky also did. Mother was apt to let herself into their house before breakfast, and had a penchant for giving the children all sorts of pets – terrapins, guinea pigs and a hamster, most of which she ended up looking after! I seem to remember the hamster escaping in her cottage and living in the sofa for months. As it only came out at night they couldn't catch it.

Ian Barron recalls a time when he talked to my mother. He said he remembered the terrapins in the bath at the barn conversion at Ringletts! (They had to be taken out and let loose on the bathroom floor every time someone took a bath.) He says: "That reminds me of a famous remark Daphne made when I was visiting her there – 'Mrs Holmes, how do you manage?' (A bit cheeky as I was meaning to say, 'how do you manage financially?') Your mother replied in her dismissive way, 'the Lord provides,' and Hugo, who was standing behind me said, 'yes - and *I* am the Lord!'

Their eldest son, Robert was born on 20th July 1969, the day the American astronauts, uttering the immortal words, 'One small step for man, one giant step for mankind', landed on the moon. Since then Robert, and his wife Ouvrielle, have taken their own giant steps with their 'Grobag' empire. Ouvrielle, who was born on the 11th December 1967, and Robert now have four children, Sam, 21st December 1996, Lucy, 30th March 1999, William, 18th October 2003 and Edward, 6th March 2006.

Robert attended prep school in Eastbourne, followed by Eastbourne College before going to Art College and university. He then took up graphic design, eventually moving to Salcombe to start his own business - but soon became involved (not always voluntarily!) with his father's various enterprises. At one time Hugo and Vicky owned the houseboats in Salcombe harbour, a water sports centre, a restaurant and a night club in Kingsbridge which Robert still runs very successfully.

Robert and Ouvrielle were married in the chancel of Lincoln Cathedral with the wedding guests sitting in the choir stalls. It was a lovely private wedding and when we emerged we walked into the flash of dozens of cameras held by a group of Japanese tourists. They obviously thought we were very special! Which of course we were!

I have special memories of Robert's best man's speech when he described a wedding Robert attended in Denver, USA. For some reason Robert persuaded one of the bridesmaids to swap clothes with him. He then descended to the hotel lobby, dressed as a bridesmaid, only to find a 'Gay' Convention checking in whose members greeted him with enthusiasm! We were led to understand that Robert legged it back to the wedding as fast as he could!

Ben, who was born on 22nd January 1972, joined Robert at prep school before going on to Winchester, where, amongst other things, he built, (with a little help!) a two-men hovercraft. Ben won scholarships to both Winchester and Eton but was sent to Winchester because academically his parents thought it is far better. He also became interested in theatricals and, on leaving school, spent a year in Exeter as a trainee stage manager, followed by Exeter University where he shared a house with Robert and friends. He then went on to enter the world of film and television. He was involved with the Edinburgh Fringe Festival one year, where, I understand they were very successful.

Ben has, for as long as I can remember, worn baseball hats – at all times, though I don't know if he wears one to bed! He also, like me, *hates* losing and once when he joined Michael and me in France, we played scrabble. Poor Michael had a terrible time with the pair of us and ending up cheating so that *he* didn't win.

Ben married Nevena, (born on 3rd February 1973), and who, at the time of their marriage, was chaperone to one of the children in the original Harry Potter film. It was a beautiful wedding in a wonderful old castle.   Robert was prepared with baseball hats for the reception and just as Ben got to his feet to make his speech we were all invited to reach under the tables where black bin bags were hidden with baseball caps embroidered with 'Ben & Nev'. We all enjoyed the joke.

They have since had their first son, Harry, who was born on 13th November 2004, and second, Matty arriving on 25th October 2006.

Sailing

Hugo's first boat was a Graduate, a twelve foot dinghy, which he raced at the Eastbourne Sailing club – very successfully I should add. Years later, fed up with finding crews, he and Ian Barron changed to Lasers, single handed dinghies.

Vicky's parents owned a lovely house in Salcombe with fabulous views out to sea. Hugo, Ian and their respective families spent many a happy summer holiday staying at this house. Both Ian and Hugo towed their boats down and held private races between each other. Robert was the starter for these races, known as 'The Potty Race'. Upon enquiring what 'The Potty Race' was, Ian explained that Robert would stand up on the hill above the bay waving a white child's potty and when the two boats were roughly in line he would drop the potty as a signal for the race to begin!

Other Interests

My brother was one of those people who was very enthusiastic about trying anything – the only problem was that he became bored just as quickly as his enthusiasm had grown. He tried shooting, skiing, wind surfing and even thought about going into politics. Hugo decided to become a Liberal MP, unfortunately when the Liberals didn't accept his application immediately he gave up that idea too. He previously stood, unsuccessfully, for the local council. It was a shame he wasn't accepted for either post as his amazing brain and his ability to absorb facts would have made him a fine MP and would certainly have kept his mind stretched.

Hugo did enjoy a drink or two and Ian recalls the time my brother visited them in their home the evening before the two families departed for their annual Salcombe pilgrimage. Unfortunately, Hugo went a bit overboard with their wine, drove off, crashed his car, with his boat on a trailer behind it, and reappeared at Ian's an hour later with his teeth knocked out. Ian was a Harley Street dentist at that stage and the two of them were forced to make a dash very early the following morning from Eastbourne to London to repair Hugo's teeth!

I recall one episode when we invited Hugo and Vicky to join us for the Hunt Ball at Cowdray House, where Jo was working. They arrived to stay, brought their luggage into the house only to find that Vicky had not packed Hugo's white tie dress suit trousers. Upon his remonstrating with her, she blandly said, "But you didn't tell me you needed them." We eventually borrowed another pair which were far too big and had to held up with braces and a belt!

Hugo's Career

After his brief spell with the accountants in London, and the ice-cream van episode, my brother settled down as an Estate Agent, first with Oakden & Co., working hard to pass his Royal Institute of Chartered Surveyors exams. Later, bored with Estate Agency, he went into property development and built several blocks of flats and houses in Eastbourne, before returning to Estate Agency and starting his own firm with a partner, under the name of Holmes and Leadbitter. They successfully expanded the company to twelve offices before selling out during the Estate Agency boom when banks and insurance companies were buying up dozens of individual firms.

The family moved to Devon, where they bought a small farm and Hugo and Vicky took up sheep farming, along with the odd Pot-bellied pig or two. Again he became bored, the farm was sold and they moved to Salcombe, buying the family house where they had spent so many holidays.

Hugo became the tycoon again, starting in Salcombe with the houseboat business, but becoming ill a year later with throat cancer, which he beat, for a while. With a second lease of life, he bought a restaurant in Kingsbridge and created a water sports centre in Salcombe. Sadly the cancer reappeared in his lungs and he died in late October in 1995 at the age of fifty-one.

Although both he and Anton, my former husband, who died at the age of fifty-six, did not live on into old age they both had very full lives doing, seeing and achieving a great deal. In other words they filled it up rather than stretching it out.

Robert's picture

One interesting thing happened much later, in 2008 in fact. I have inherited my father's psychic ability and was lying in bed one night when absolutely clearly in my mind my brother came through. He looked younger than when he died. He 'told' me all sorts of things, which I admit I could have imagined, but the one thing I didn't know came at the end. My brother told me to tell Robert that the picture connected with him wasn't moving, or going crooked because somebody was bumping into it, the picture was moving because my brother was trying to let them know he was still around.

Remembering the watercolours Robert had painted when he was young, I instantly thought Hugo was referring to one of them. When I finally got hold of Ouvrielle, Robert was out, I told her about my experience and she immediately said, "Oh, that picture taken of Robert when he was at school – it is always going crooked. Hold on a minute, I straightened again only this morning, I'll go and check it now." She went to check, taking the phone with her, "It is crooked again, and there is nobody else in the house!" Strange? After Rob 'talked' to his father it stopped moving, until around the time of my sister's death, when all the pictures in Rob's youngest son's room seemed to have moved, and it was impossible it could have been done by the baby as he was too little. Rob and I decided it was probably his father asking why we had sent his sister Jo over to the other side!

CHAPTER 9
EDINBURGH AND ATHOL CRESCENT

Arriving In Edinburgh

I was seventeen when my mother put me on the coach for Edinburgh to begin four terms at College. We had chosen the short Household and Institutional Management course. Mother had never learnt to do anything useful in the house and decided I ought to.

My aunt met me at the coach station in Edinburgh accompanied by her two 'boys', a couple of black and white mongrels called Benji and Barney. My father referred to Nathalie and the dogs as, Benji, Barney and Barmy! He was absolutely correct, she was quite nutty. I became their 'cousin Anna' and found it very embarrassing to hear my aunt addressing the dogs with, "Come on Benji, Barney, get up on your cousin Anna's lap as we sat down on a bus.

Aunt Nathalie and 'The Boys'

My aunt lived just off the Haymarket at the end of Princess Street. She owned a basement flat in one of the tall tenement blocks which were built round a central garden system, divided by five foot stone walls so that each basement had its own little garden. The flat itself was mostly store cupboards, one of which was stacked floor to ceiling with tins of dog food and Nestle's cream, and the only useable rooms were two at the front and two at the rear. All the others were windowless. Some years before I moved in with Aunt N, we had gone up to stay with her as a family. I'd better explain that my aunt was reasonably tall and had a very deep penetrating voice. On this occasion Aunt Nathalie suddenly announced at 5.25 pm that she had run out of food for her dogs.

"Oh, my dears," she bellowed out, "I've realised I haven't any food for the 'boys'. I'll just run down to the shop and get some."

My father being a reasonable man said, "But Nathalie you've got a whole storeroom full of tins."

"Oh, no," she said in her authoritative voice, "I can't use that, that's there in case there's a *nuclear* war and I'm killed!"

My father quietly added, "Well I'm sure you've taught them how to use a tin opener."

Another lovely story connecting Uncle Hugo and Aunt Nathalie was when my uncle retired from The Royal Scots. At the time of his retirement he was based at the Regiment's Headquarters in Edinburgh Castle, where three of his dogs are buried in the tiny cemetery for dogs. The Regiment gave a dinner for him, inviting the elite of the Regiment and a fair sprinkling of important residents of Edinburgh. Stupidly my uncle also asked Aunt Nathalie to attend. It was a full evening dress affair with the ladies expected to wear long gowns, however my aunt was going through one of her mean moods and refused to buy a new dress and turned up wearing a cocktail dress with a, very obvious, long nightdress underneath! I don't think Uncle Hugo ever forgave her for that.

Living with Aunt Nathalie

I moved in with her and was given the front bedroom. Her room was at the back next to the sitting room where the dogs slept. One day she asked me to hang out their blankets. I couldn't believe it when I shook out *fourteen* blankets most of which had holes chewed in them when the 'boys' burrowed their way in and ate their way out!

The back door was never shut. This was in case the 'boys' wanted to rush out day or night. Aunt N had built up a pile of earth in the corner of the garden next to one of the walls and whenever there was a noise, these two hysterical animals would rush out barking frantically, jump on the wall and rush round from garden to garden. The neighbours didn't appreciate it.

Aunt Nathalie was one of those infuriating people who would argue the leg off a donkey. It didn't matter what you said she would disagree. She decided to go to Edinburgh University when she was in her forties, I think it was to annoy mother who was much cleverer than Aunt N had ever been. I remember her tutor saying sorrowfully to my parents that when my aunt was in his class, he didn't know if she was taking it or he was.

She was also addicted to visiting the local police station with 'things' she had found. I know she was very upset with the reaction of the duty policeman when she arrived with a pigeon, which she insisted was a lost homing pigeon 'prew, prewing' under her arm and the 'boys' tugging at their leads pulling her up to the front desk. As the duty officer looked up he saw her advancing and let out an expletive and a 'Jesus Christ! What has she brought in now?' It was quite a long time before she took anything else in.

My aunt used to drink Dubonnet, although later in life I think it was whisky she packed away. She also smoked 'Craven A' cigarettes and would often talk with one of these tucked into the corner of her mouth.

My brother used to talk about the time he was staying with her. He was driving her car with Aunt N in the passenger seat. Needless to say, she began to argue with Hugo. Suddenly as they were travelling along, she reached across switched the engine off and threw the keys out of the window! The car finally came to a halt some way from where the keys landed in the long grass. It took them quite a while before they found them with each accusing the other and getting crosser and crosser all the time.

The Royal Forth Yacht Club

I joined the Royal Forth Yacht Club and very rapidly made many friends. Mostly I sailed with the university crowd, but one evening, the owner of a 'fifteen square metre', thirty foot yacht and an 'out and out' sailing machine, needed a crew. Young Jimmy, who was probably about the same age as me was sent ashore to recruit someone. I volunteered and remained with them as third hand for the rest of my stay in Edinburgh. I heard later that when 'Uncle Willy', as we called him, saw me in a very long sailing jacket with apparently nothing on underneath, he almost put to sea without either Jimmy or me. Because my shorts were so *short* I became known as 'Miss nae nicks', (Miss No Knickers). One summer Sunday evening, when I climbed off a bus in the middle of Princess Street, wearing my sailing jacket and the offending shorts, there were crows of disapproval from the sedate Edinburgh residents.

I was invited to crew on a Dragon owned by the premier helmsman in Scotland when Willy was away. Naturally I was delighted, until the owner told me I was foredeck hand and therefore responsible for putting up, taking down and 'packing' the spinnaker in between circuits of the buoys. In shock I stepped backwards and fell straight into Grantham Harbour where we were still moored. Without pausing to draw breath, the helmsman reached over the side, plucked me out of the water, dumped me on deck and announced that we hadn't time for me to get changed and off we set to compete in that afternoon's Dragon race.

Kind Uncle Willy actually allowed me to race his 'fifteen square' in the ladies race. He and Jimmy were *my* crew for the afternoon. I had never helmed a keel boat before and treated it like a racing dinghy, cutting in on the buoys and calling for 'water' on the mark. We won, but the poor man came back with more grey hairs than he'd started with!

We did laugh when Edward Heath, a one time Prime Minister, tied his boat, Flying Cloud, against the harbour wall. Unfortunately for him he secured it on far too short ropes and when the tide went out, it left his yacht hanging against the harbour wall.

Poached Eggs and Spinach

Most evenings I went out with student friends, but one particular evening I did not have anywhere to go and Aunt N pounced. I needed an early night she said. I agreed.

"Do you like cooked spinach?"

"No," I replied. It was the boiled stinging nettles that had put me off.

"Do you like poached eggs?"

I do like eggs but am not fond of poached ones as I prefer my eggs cooked hard and so I told her I didn't. So what did I get for dinner? Spinach with a poached egg on top!

I retired to bed at about 7.30 pm with a good book and was feeling drowsy, when at about 9.0 pm, the door opened and in walked Aunt N.

"What! Aren't you asleep yet?"

She could see I wasn't and she disappeared, coming back with a glass of *warm* milk and a slice of very heavy fruit cake she'd made.

"It's a long time since you had your supper, you must be hungry," she said, handing me the glass and cake which I duly ate and drank while she stood over me. Off she went, but about fifteen minutes later she arrived *again.*

"You can't possibly go to sleep on a full stomach she boomed at me, "Get up and come for a walk with the 'boys' and I."

So much for an early night!

Athol Crescent

I loved the Edinburgh College of Domestic Science which was a cross between a finishing school for foreign girls, those who would never have to earn their own living and the ones who were making a career out of catering, dieticians or other useful occupations. I do remember one teacher chastising one of the Argentineans, who was much more interested in shoes and clothes than nutrition and hygiene, by saying that although she might never have to pick up a duster herself, she'd get more respect from her staff if she could demonstrate she was capable of doing the job herself.

I enjoyed the sewing and upholstery classes and really got into the cookery, except the day we prepared stuffed sheep's head. We had to brush the teeth of the half head before stuffing the skull - Uuugh! Then there was the haggis – I've never liked haggis since I know what goes into them and also the classic afternoon when we had to make white puddings, similar to black puddings but made with oatmeal which gives them a whiter colour, using the small intestine as the skin. My friend, Miss Hartley, we were always called *Miss* So-and-so, anyway Phillipa Hartley attached one end of the intestine to one tap and I attached the other end to another and we turned the water on to clean it out. Needless to say it burst and sprayed water everywhere.

I think laundry was my least favourite lesson, especially as we had to bring in items to wash and iron. Everything my aunt gave me was so stained and grubby that I never got round to the ironing because I was too busy trying to get the marks out of the tablecloth, or whatever little joy she'd given me that day!

In our final term we were sent to Lorne House, one of the residential colleges, to do six weeks 'on house'. In other words we were unpaid cooks, cleaners and bottle washers. Phillipa, a wonderful nun from Ireland and me formed our small team. I'm sure we drove our tutor mad, especially when I managed to break off the handle that controlled the huge mixer when it was beating at its fastest rate. We were then forced to form a circle round it, for the two days before it was mended, to catch stray potatoes as they were thrown out by centrifugal force!

Towards the end of my stay at Athol Crescent, I was invited to a 'June Ball' at Oxford. Unfortunately it was the day before I did my final Nutrition and Hygiene exam. I was desperate to go and went to ask the principal for permission because, although I would not completely miss the exam, I would be an hour late. I'll always remember the principal, who was new, asking me if I'd ever been to a ball in either Oxford or Cambridge before, upon replying that I hadn't, she promptly said that of course I must go as it was much better for my education than doing the exam, which I could re-sit if I failed. What a forward thinking woman she was.

I missed my flight and arrived back at college for the last hour and a quarter of the three hour exam - and passed it!

On one classic wet afternoon several of us students went to the cinema. It was a dreadful flea pit of a place but they didn't deserve what we did. One of our group had a bottle of live moths in his pocket. He waited until the 'black and white' film was underway and opened the bottle. The moths flew straight up the beam of light to the camera. As they neared the projection box their shadows got larger and larger on the screen. Chaos was caused because there was no way the attendants could deal with them. The moment they turned on the house lights the moths disappeared and then when they turned *off* the main lights and put the film back on, the moths came out of the shadows and attacked the projector again. As we were just about the only people in the cinema that afternoon we were thrown out!

Frederick Street

After enduring, it was mutual for both of us I believe, Aunt Nathalie's company for six months, I moved in with four other girls into a flat immediately above the *Aperitif Restaurant* in Frederick Street, just off Princess Street. (It is no longer there.) The quickest way to college was down Rose Street, which runs parallel with Princess Street. In those days it was just one pub after another and was pretty seedy. I really enjoyed living in Frederick Street, but unfortunately it was some friends of mine from Eastbourne that caused us to get evicted. Angus Graham, who always reminded mother of the White Rabbit from Alice in Wonderland, dressed up in some of my clothes and pranced down Princess Street. Nowadays nobody would even glance at him but things were different in 1960. Then we held a party and several cushions were thrown out of the window on to the heads of some of the elite guests arriving to dine at the very expensive restaurant below. The owners were *not* amused and I moved again to a smaller flat with one other girl.

Boyfriends in Edinburgh

My first boyfriend was a charming, but an unreliable American called Clifford Shooter. He was in Edinburgh studying medicine like most of the friends I had there - either that or training to become vets. I actually had few close friends from Athol Crescent as none of them had similar interests.

I remember one time when Cliff came to visit us in Eastbourne we decided to teach him how to play bridge. He was very serious about it and at one point when he left the room to go to the loo, mother 'packed' his hand with all the picture cards. Poor fellow, he didn't know what to call and slowly pushed the bidding up and up and it was only when we laughed that he found out what we'd done. He was furious and refused to play again.

Then there was Martin Hubbard. Although he wasn't really a boyfriend, he was far fonder of me than I was of him. Years later I felt very sad about the way I treated him. Martin introduced me to Georgette Heyer, which was to become one of my favourite authors.

Sandy, an Australian came next. He was the most fantastic ballroom dancer and always wanted to be first up on the dance floor. After him was David Cameron, who was probably the nicest of the lot. Later he arranged for me to meet up with his brother who was stationed in Singapore with the Cameron Highlanders.

Not long before I left Edinburgh I received a phone call from my mother and Maggie Connelly, head receptionist at the Cavendish Hotel. Maggie had met her future husband at the hotel. Bill was currently in the Merchant Navy, but was planning to retire from the navy and do a shore job. He found one in Hong Kong. Poor Maggie obviously thought that Hong Kong was a very uncivilised part of the world and phoned to ask me if I would go and visit her over there. I immediately agreed and my mother bought me a *one-way ticket* on the P & O liner the Chusan for early the following October.

A year and a half after I'd gone to Edinburgh, I left for my final summer holiday at home, and although I didn't know at the time, I would never live at home again. When I eventually returned to England, over three years later my father had died, I had married and given birth to my first son Simon.

81

CHAPTER 10
HONG KONG

Go and See the World

I knew nobody on the Chusan, the ship which was to be my home for the next four weeks. Mother took me to Tilbury Docks to sail to Hong Kong. I was only just nineteen at the time and found myself sharing a cabin with an older lady – poor woman! I got the upper berth and, as I never went to bed until much later than this unlucky woman, I am sure she didn't enjoy the trip half as much as I did.

There were a number of other girls on board, some of whom were travelling together, others on their own and some going home to their parents, however we all joined forces and had a whale of a time. One of the girls was Gill Montserrat, the niece of the famous author.

The worst experience of the cruise was sailing through the Bay of Biscay when we encountered a gale. Most people succumbed to severe seasickness and remained in their cabins. After an initial bout of feeling unwell I spent the day on deck and was one of the very few, including the staff, able to face dinner in the evening. En route to Hong Kong we docked in Gibraltar, Port Said, Aden, Bombay, Colombo, Penang, and Singapore.

One of the other passengers was a charming Indian doctor, who had been living in England for a number of years. He managed to contact his family in Bombay (now Mumbai), and arranged for them to meet the ship where they invited a group of us girls to their home, which was sumptuous, and also showed us some of the sights of Bombay. They were obviously a very wealthy high caste family and we were treated like royalty.

Three of us were nearly thrown off the ship at Bombay. The Captain warned us that if we were caught swimming in the pool on 1ˢᵗ Class decks again we would be sent home! So we went underground instead, visiting the young officers in their cabins and seeing parts of the ship we were not supposed to go, like the engine room.

In Penang we had to say farewell to one of the girls who was going home to join her parents on their rubber plantation. Like the charming Indian family in Bombay, they also entertained and gave us a wonderful guided tour before departing for Singapore, our final stop before Hong Kong.

David Cameron, my Edinburgh boyfriend, had written to his brother to warn him of my arrival and he arrived at the dock with two other officers and invited me to choose two girls to join us for three memorable days in Singapore. Each morning they arrived at the dock and swept us off. They entertained us at their mess in Changi and took us to have tea at the Raffles Hotel. We also visited Boogie Street to sample the food sold on the outdoor stalls. It was years later that I found out that most of the 'beautiful women' strolling in this part of Singapore were not actually women at all! They were exotic transvestites who must have fooled many a sailor.

Then it was on to Hong Kong where Maggie Connelly, now married to Bill Gardner, was waiting to meet me. It was sad to say good bye to all the young officers on the ship but a new life beckoned me.

Hong Kong

Maggie had invited some young men to meet me and it was only a couple of days before I joined the Royal Hong Kong Yacht Club. At that time the Club was situated on Kellett Island and was joined to Hong Kong Island by a causeway, which formed part of a typhoon shelter, a sheltered area of water like a walled harbour. (Since then the authorities have filled it in when they built the tunnel under the harbour to link the Island with Kowloon on the mainland) Except when a typhoon was raging the shelter was mostly home for dozens of small sampans on which whole families lived. The boats and yachts belonging to the club's members were also moored in there. For the sampan families there was no sanitation available and so everything was just chucked into the water which was, when you could *see* it, a filthy dark brown colour with everything from fruit and vegetable peelings to human waste floating on the surface. It was absolutely *disgusting!* A year or so later, Anton, who was by then, my husband, fell into the water when he was trying to get on board a yacht to go sailing. He said there was even a dead pig floating around that day! The skipper, the infamous Don Brown, absolutely refused to let him on board until he'd been into the yacht club and had a shower.

Don, a Quantas flight engineer, was one of the people invited to meet me on my first evening in Hong Kong and he came with a man called Alan Stevenson. I never knew why Maggie had asked these two as they were both completely unsuitable. Don was thirty-nine at the time and Alan was gay! However they did sponsor me into joining the yacht club. It was very elite in those days and was threatened with losing its Royal Charter if they didn't open the membership up to Chinese and Asians. While I was there nobody other than white people were members.

Meeting Anton

After I had been in Hong Kong for about three weeks I decided to go and visit some of the other girls who had sailed out from England with me. It was now late November and quite cold in the evenings. I went round to their apartment wearing a tweed suit and found them all dressed in their finery and having a party. I think they were a little embarrassed at not inviting me. The room was full of young army officers from the barracks at Lyemun, which was at the far end of the island. One of them caught my eye immediately, Anton Emmerton who was with John Kistner, both 2nd Lieutenants in the RASC. Anton had an infectious laugh and was, as he always did, keeping the whole room laughing.

Anton, John and I left the party together. As we got into the lift they noticed a sign saying, 'Do not jump in the lift.' It was very curious as to why it said that, but of course it was just the thing for two inebriated young men to promptly do. Needless to say, the lift stopped between two floors and we were stuck. Having rung the internal bell to make it known the lift had broken, we sat down on the filthy floor and played 'spoof' with coins. An hour later, when we were released, Anton asked me to go out with him. I responded by asking him whether he sailed and upon his replying no he didn't, I told him I didn't have time! Anton took up sailing and from then on his life and career were dominated by boats.

I think it is fair to talk about Anton here. He was a very talented man. An excellent artist and later wrote had several very exciting novels published. He was witty and good fun and very attractive – but he was very difficult to live with. His attitude towards me when we were on our own was so different from the face he showed other people. Years later I came to the conclusion he should never have married and in this I was seconded by Anton's second wife, Leslie Clark.

The Royal Hong Kong Yacht Club

Soon after I arrived in Hong Kong the yacht club held its annual 'Pirates Ball'. Everybody dressed up as pirates and having heard about what a fun evening it was, I naturally was very keen to attend. Unfortunately, Don Brown had invited me out for dinner on that evening and I had accepted. Then another young man asked me to go to the Pirates Ball. I'm afraid I phoned Don and left a message for him, telling him a fib, but he didn't get my message and so both he and the young man arrived at the same time to take me out. It was so embarrassing! In the end we all, including Maggie and Bill, went to the ball and apart from Don giving me some nasty looks, everyone had a great time.

The yacht club boasted its own two lane bowling alley with automatic pin setting - that is if we could get one of the Chinese staff to sit at the end and replace the pins as we knocked them down!

Mostly I sailed Enterprise sailing dinghies, but on one ghastly Saturday afternoon I was invited to sail as foredeck hand on a Dragon. It had been the number one Dragon in the Colony until it was bought by an American, Bill Crum. He was an awful helmsman, admittedly he had a dreadful squint which may have been the reason he couldn't steer straight. It was the 'Round the Island Race', which meant sailing right round the island of Hong Kong. The first leg headed towards the main part of the city and the Star Ferry berths and as it was completely down wind, we hoisted the spinnaker. With the spinnaker up it is essential to keep the wind behind, but Bill was unable to do so. Every time I got the sail set he altered course causing the spinnaker pole to slam up against the forestay and nearly knocking me overboard. I then altered the pole to the other corner of the triangular sail and seconds later the same thing happened. After changing the spinnaker half a dozen times I took it down because it was too dangerous! By this time the other yachts were disappearing into the distance.

We sailed on gradually losing ground on those ahead. After about three hours or so while the third member of the crew and I kept our heads down, there was a tremendous thump and we looked up to find that Bill had hit a seventy foot junk amidships! – creating a large hole in the side of the Chinese vessel. Dragons are equipped with a very sharp pointed metal bow. Untangling ourselves we sailed on with Bill saying that if they wanted any money they could come to the Yacht Club. They never did of course.

A couple of years later, Bill mysteriously died in a huge fire at his home. It was only then that I was told he had been head of the mafia in the Far East, peddling drugs, women and whatever else he was into. I don't think many people mourned him.

The meal in Wanchai

One evening after we had been sailing, we decided to go out for a meal in Wanchai. I don't know what kind of Chinese meal it was, but we were served with very thin strips of meat which we dunked in water boiling in a sort of a small trough around a tall burner in the middle. We then dipped the cooked meat into egg and vegetables - I think. During the evening quantities of San Miguel Beer was drunk and I became desperate to go to the 'loo'. I was directed into the kitchen where behind a curtain there was just a trough, almost like an open drain, in the floor. That was the 'loo'.

Inside the Yacht Club

In the main lounge, over the bar was a particularly dreadful mural. It depicted several yachts sailing. After quite a few alcoholic beverages we decided to 'make it better'. Using menu cards and other bits and pieces, we added sails and numbers to mimic boats at the yacht club. We thought it looked great but someone had been watching through the window and we all got into trouble with the committee.

At the club there were two small flats which were let out to a couple of members. One was Don Brown. His bed was a typical Chinese bed with a wooden frame and slats just laid across with the mattress on top. We all knew he was taking a woman out for dinner, and although he was engaged to a charming South African girl, we guessed he would bring his date back to his room afterwards. While he was out we crept up and removed the slats and carefully rearranged his bed. Hiding in the flat opposite, we waited for Don to return and throw himself, and his date, onto the bed. It promptly collapsed and great cries of rage were heard coming from the room. Killing ourselves with laughter we almost created a tragedy when Don picked up the main perpetrator and threw him down the stairs!

More about Anton

When I first met Anton he was driving an Austin Healey. He and John Kistner were very wild and used to have races round the island at night. Heaven knows how they managed not to kill themselves, or anyone else. They also raced up and down the multi-story car park which terrified any unfortunate person who was trying to get his or her car out.

Anton and I began to go out seriously and it wasn't too many months before we decided to get married. On the evening of our engagement we went down to the Yacht club to celebrate and met, for the first time, Tony Fleming and his fiancée Mary. We had planned to go apartment hunting – I had already moved out from Bill and Maggie's and was living in a bed sit on Kowloon side. It just happened that Tony was moving out of a small flat on the island and agreed that I could take it on, so instead of house hunting we all had dinner together and it was the beginning of friendships and many career connections that were to last until Anton's death over thirty five years later.

Tony's flat had the most wonderful views over the city and the harbour. Two Australian girls, who were completely mad, moved in with me until Anton and I got married. There are several things I remember about this apartment. We had a Chinese Amah living with us and her accommodation was limited to the extreme. Her bed was a tile shelf in a room the size of a small cupboard just off the kitchen. The other things I recall were the cockroaches. They were enormous and would come out at night and stalk around the floors, only scurrying back into the walls when you put a light on. There was nothing we could do to get rid of them as they lived throughout the skyscraper we lived in.

Our cars

Anton was 'persuaded' by his senior officer to sell his Austin Healey to cover his mess bills. I can't remember what sort of car he bought then but later we acquired an old black 'Mayflower' which had been owned by a Chinese and was upholstered in flowery chintz. It went – sort of, but at a later stage, the apartment we were in was on a steep hill and the car would only go up it in reverse. We would do a quick three point turn at the bottom of the hill and drive at speed backwards to where the road flattened out and do another quick turn and go forwards again.

There was one famous occasion when we were heading towards the Yacht Club and had to make a U-turn on to the road running alongside the harbour. Suddenly a wheel rolled past us and with surprise Anton questioned where it could have come from – then a *bang* and a terrible scraping sound was heard from the undercarriage of our car – it was ours!

On another night Anton and John were cruising past the concrete building where the American naval military police waited in case their servicemen caused trouble in any of the waterfront bars. Anton had taken with him a 'thunder flash', a simulated hand grenade used for training purposes and as John slowed down to drive past the 'Snowballs' building, (Snowball being a name given to the MP's because of their all white uniform), Anton pulled the pin and rolled this thing in amongst the Americans. As he and John sped away there was a huge bang and the military police staggered out covered in black dust. I feel quite sure that if they had caught Anton and John they would have been very seriously dealt with. Fortunately nobody was hurt as it was a pretty silly thing to do.

Another time Anton followed a night exercise being held by the Northumberland Fusiliers also armed with his thunder flashes. It was pitch dark and so he was not only able to closely follow small groups of men but to wreak havoc with these same fake grenades and totally wreck the entire exercise.

The Northumberland Fusiliers were sharing Lyemun Barracks and would enjoy Mess nights with Anton and John, who were in the RASC, and on one occasion, one of the wild Northumberland's climbed on the table, grabbed the big ceiling fan and hung on while it turned slowly. Gradually the two blades he was holding bent lower and lower until he fell off in a heap onto the fully laden table smashing glasses and crockery to the cheers of most of the young men.

Anton and his Chinese Soldiers

His platoon was based at Victoria Barracks in the heart of the city and close to Government House. Anton was responsible for training Chinese and Ghurkha soldiers to drive three ton lorries and jeeps. He found it almost impossible to teach the Ghurkhas as they had no road sense at all. Tell them not to *exceed* 30 mph in the city and they would stick at 30 mph through street markets, in crowds, oblivious to the road conditions. Anton was also fond of 'driver training' to Shekko beach for the afternoon where they would all swim and sunbathe before 'driver training' back to the barracks.

At this time, he had a Chinese soldier, called Lau Si Kau. He was Anton's office batman and, among other duties, made his coffee. On one occasion, when trying to get a phone line via the switchboard manned by British girls, Anton became impatient and decided to have a cup of coffee. "Lau Si Kau", he shouted and at that moment the switchboard answered with an irate woman saying, "How dare you! Don't you call me a lousy cow!" He and his Chinese assistant had to go and prove he wasn't being rude to her but just wanted some coffee

Married Life

I was working at Everett Travel, immediately opposite the Peninsular Hotel on Kowloon side when we got married. Initially I was involved with sea bookings before being switched to air. My boss gave me one week to learn how to do flight bookings! I used to work out the first carrier and then go across to the Peninsula Hotel to meet with the airline agency and get them to write up the whole ticket.

One of my clearest memories is the humidity in the summer in Hong Kong - 90 degrees of heat and 90 % humidity. Everett Travel was less than half a mile from the Star Ferry but if I didn't take a taxi, I was dripping with perspiration when I arrived at work.

I had an amazing experience while still involved with sea bookings. An American came into the office and, I later realised he was teasing, said he'd got a boat and would I like to see it. I thought it was probably a freighter with a small number of passenger cabins so I said yes. Later on that day I went with some other people to the harbour and climbed on board an American naval launch. We were taken right outside the harbour to the USS Ranger which was far too big to get into Hong Kong harbour. Not a passenger ship at all, but very interesting. As it was an American vessel it was 'dry' and we were offered coffee or Coca-Cola. No wonder the sailors got so drunk when they came ashore.

My First Wedding

Anton was a 2nd Lieutenant in the RASC and so the wedding was naturally army orientated. Colonel Thompson gave me away and a guard of honour with eight brother officers formed an arch with their dress swords for us to walk under as we left the church.

We held the reception at Lyemun Barracks and our honeymoon was on a *very* small two berth yacht on which we planned to sail round the numerous islands off Hong Kong. Unfortunately, for us, it was the beginning of the typhoon season and with typhoon warnings going up, we couldn't stray very far. We were lucky that the typhoon veered away and we were able to complete our week's sailing. My clearest memory of the trip was diving into the warm sea during the night to deter the mosquitoes. I discovered they didn't like wet salty bodies!

Typhoon Wanda

Six weeks later Typhoon Wanda hit the Colony. Anton was on duty and so I went to stay with Colonel Thompson and his wife. The typhoon was one of the biggest ever experienced in Hong Kong as it hit the island absolutely dead on. Gusts of wind up to 170 mph tore up trees, destroyed buildings and caused ships to break away from their moorings. Most of the big ships left the harbour prior to the storm, especially all naval vessels. Later a large container ship was found washed a mile and a half inshore and lay abandoned among the paddy fields. The storm occurred, not only at high tide, but a spring tide as well and so the waves were huge.

One of the large Star Ferries moored in a typhoon shelter broke away and a Chinese ferry operator went out to it and literally drove up and down so that it didn't crash into the junks and sampans sheltering from the wind. The loss of life and damage would have been enormous if it hadn't been for this brave man.

While Anton was on duty with his sergeant, Mick Munn, Mick's dog needed to go out. As soon as the dog left the building it was quite literally pushed along on its bottom by the force of the gale. Anton and Mick had to crawl on their stomachs, as it was impossible to stand up at the height of the storm, to reach the dog which was by this time pinned up against a chain link fence, poor thing.

The strangest part of the experience was when the eye of the storm passed over the Colony. The winds went almost instantly from 170 mph to nothing. Birds began to sing again and people came out to rescue their things and then half an hour later the winds went from zero to flat out again. The noise was almost inexplicable. Between the howling of the circular storm and the sound of trees, roofs, hoardings and anything that could be torn off and blown around, it was impossible to hear anything else.

One sailing friend, who lived on Lantau Island, and had come over to the Island to wait the typhoon out found, when he returned home, that all that was left of his house was a shell. The wind and sand from the beach had torn everything out and scoured the place - even stripping the paint from the walls.

Mary and Tony's Wedding

Soon after we got married, Tony and Mary tied the knot. I think that everything that could go wrong did. Firstly, Mary had a problem getting the bridesmaids dresses on time. Then, when she and the bridesmaids drove to the hairdresser on the morning of the big day, she found it was closed – they had forgotten to tell her they were taking a holiday. Tony went to the church only to find that the carefully taped music he had supplied had been accidentally wiped off by the vicar. By this time they discovered they couldn't go on their honeymoon cruise because the shipping line was on strike. They had booked flights to Manila but because of the strike were forced to fly out three days after their wedding.

After the reception, when they were driving off to go to the hotel, Anton reached into the open car they had been lent and pulled out the ignition key. Unfortunately for them they didn't notice and strangely the engine continued to run. That is until they stopped at some traffic lights and the car stalled – and they had no key to restart it. The owner managed to catch up with them with the key and they proceeded to the Repulse Bay Hotel where they opened up Mary's suitcase only to find that most of her clothes were ruined. I had put confetti in but someone else added a damp bottle of champagne straight out of the ice-bucket. The colour from the confetti had run and stained her clothes. While at the Repulse Bay Hotel for three days with not much to do, they invited us to join them for dinner one evening.

Then some shaving cream of Tony's exploded in his luggage on the airplane and ruining some of his clothes. After that, they arrived at the hotel in Manila and retired to the 'honeymoon' suite. It was anything but! There was no running water, only a wash basin attached to the wall with a bucket underneath to catch the dirty water, and no plumbing. They didn't stay at this hotel for long before managing to find a lovely hotel and enjoy what remained of their wedding plans.

My different jobs

My first job was in the Travel Agency on Kowloon side, but after we were married I went to work in a very expensive watch and clock shop on Hong Kong side. I enjoyed it and was the only European working there. It was only after I accidentally allowed someone to steal a Patek Phillipe watch that we parted company.

It was a little while before I realised that every time a Japanese person came into the shop the Chinese staff vanished. I questioned them about this and they told me they would not serve any Japanese if they could avoid it. They still remembered the atrocities of the Second World War and what had occurred in Hong Kong.

Simon

Almost ten months to the day after we got married, Simon was born in the British Military Hospital at Mount Kellett. Anton took me in at about 1.30pm and was advised to go back to work as Simon would not arrive for hours, possibly as late as midnight. (Nowadays most husbands would stay with their wives, but back then it wasn't unusual for men not to be present at the birth). At 5.00pm Mrs Thompson, the Colonel's wife phoned Anton to congratulate him on becoming a father, telling him that contrary to what the nurses thought, Simon was born at 4.45pm. I stayed in hospital for ten days, not because I was ill, but because it happened that way in those days.

Actually I was so naive about giving birth and any possible problems that about ten days before I gave birth to Simon we all went out on a large motor cruiser for the day. Everyone else went water skiing while I watched them. Years later Mary Fleming, who was a sister at the hospital, told me she had packed a bag just in case I went into labour on the boat!

Our Moves

Soon after Simon was born we were offered accommodation on board a 120ft schooner which was moored out at Clearwater Bay. She was steel hulled, square rigged on the main mast and had berths for fourteen people, plus crew. The owner, a very wealthy carpet manufacturer from America, used to sail his yacht for three months with guests he had brought out to join him and then, wherever they reached at the end of three months, he would leave his boat, return to the States and leave a skeleton crew on board. We joined Sam, a Hawaiian, to look after the boat. It was madness. Anton had to travel by dinghy to the shore, then car, then Star Ferry and then taxi to get to work at Victoria Barracks. I was alone on this huge yacht with a six week old baby, and the Hawaiian.

At first we didn't understand why we kept hearing dull thuds that seemed to come from the steel hull, especially at night, later we discovered it was dynamite being used by Chinese fishermen. They found it easier to throw dynamite into the water and scoop up the fish left floating on the surface than to fish properly. The stupid thing was they killed everything and most of the creatures went to the bottom so they wasted many, many fish.

After about two months we were back looking for accommodation on Hong Kong island and for a short time we lived with Pat and Tony Whittle, who was Simon's godfather and who was tragically drowned, years later, when rescuing someone while on holiday in Africa.

While we were living back on Hong Kong side, my brother Hugo, aged 19, arrived to stay. Mother had sent him off to Australia, but he managed to get back home quicker that I did! I think she probably paid for his airfare back. Hugo and Anton became great friends, both of them having the same daft sense of humour. They started calling each other 'Jim' – I have no idea why, but it continued until their deaths.

Hugo introduced us to the card game 'Knock' while he was with us. It is one that the grandchildren still play, and I have to admit that I refuse to play with some of them as they *always* win! I clearly remember playing with Hugo and I was almost out when I had an amazing run of luck, beat him and he threw the entire pack of cards at my head!

Our final flat was on Conduit Road on the Island and it was to this one that we had to reverse our old Mayflower car. We were there for several months before returning to England.

1. Great Grandfther, John P. Wright, Esq,W.S.

2. Great Grandmother, Anna Jessie Walker Wright

3. Col. David Aubrey Callender C.M.G.

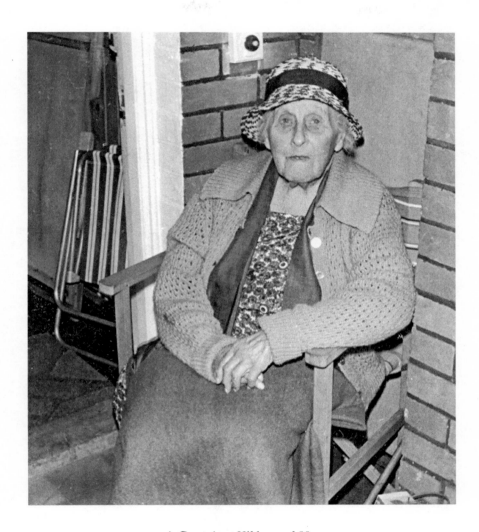

4. Great Aunt Hilda, aged 90

5. Uncle Dick on a donkey

6. Aunt Nathalie as a small child

7. "Two dripping candles!" Mother and Aunt Nathalie after their presentation at the court of George V and Queen Mary - 1927

8. Caravan with Daddy, me, Hugo and Jo

Bus behind caravan

9. The Holmes family at Piddinghoe

10. The tent that Hugo slid down in the nude at 5.30 a.m.
Aunt Natalie, Jo and me

11. Mother with neighbours outside the house in Errol

12. "Starres", Westfield near Rye about 1956

13. Brother Hugo - 1962

14 & 15. Mother and I at the Rhonllywn, Llandegly with Simon and Sean

16. Daphne Holmes on her 80th Birthday - 1988

17. Col. D. A. & Violet Callender - St. Mary's Church, Birnam, near Dunkeld

18. Col James Gordon
   Eldest surviving son Sir Alex Gordon Kt and Grace Dalrymple
   (Elder brother to David)
   Col of Militia (Kurkudbright)
   Married to Miss Hannay
   No heirs
   Was an extravagant man

19.   David Gordon of Jannylaggie
3rd Son of Sir Alex Gordon and Grace Dalrymple
Father of Mrs Chas Potter
Inventor of Portable Gas
Pioneer of Motor Carriages

20. Grace Gordon
Daughter of David Gordon of Jannylaggie and Agnes Hyslop of Lockend
Married Charles Potter, Ernsdale, Lancs
Sister of W Gordon of Culvennan

21.
William Gordon of Culvennan
Eldest Son of David Gordon of Jannylaggie and Agnes Hyslop of Lockend
Mother of Mrs Charles Potter
Father of David Gordon of Culvennan, Lt Rifle Brigade

CHAPTER 11

BACK IN ENGLAND

February 1964

We arrived home courtesy of the RAF in February and it was *cold.*
Simon was eight months old. He was a good baby, a little round lovely
child who laughed and smiled at everyone.

Upon arrival we first went to stay with my mother, my father
having died in March the previous year. I can say here that when
mother read Anton's cards, (fortune telling), she definitely did not take
to him and their mutual dislike continued for the rest of both their
lives. However, mother being mother was very generous and gave us
her car because, without it, we were unable to travel. Of course it was
not the sort of car Anton would have chosen so it wasn't long before he
traded it in for something different.

After a short time we drove down to stay with Dolly, Anton's
mother and his step-father, Dennis Manning, in Gillingham, Dorset.
They were both very welcoming but it was later that I realised that Dolly
was very possessive of her son. Poor old Den, he was lovely, but Dolly
would have always put Anton first, followed by Janice, her daughter.
Her first husband, Leslie St John Emmerton, had gone missing during
the Second World War. He had been a Spitfire pilot who had never
been found after he disappeared over Java. It was years before Dolly
was persuaded by Den to marry him. He would have loved to have had
children of his own but by then it was too late.

Naturally my mother was very upset that we should only spend a few days with her but stayed on and on with Dolly and Den. Anton not unnaturally wanted to go out with his old friends Richard Hyde, his brother-in-law; Anthony Stickland and numerous other former rugby playing friends. In those days the young men would meet up at the pub on Friday nights, then Saturday lunchtime, Saturday evening and again at lunch on Sunday. The wives were not included. I put up with this for a while and then finally dug my feet in. I did not see why I should stay in with my in-laws night after night and he should go out. I'm afraid it caused a terrible row when I told Anton that he could go on Friday but if he wanted to meet up with his friends on the Saturday evening, he could either take me or he wasn't going. Dolly was furious with me and told me I should allow him to go. I was really angry as I had never before been treated as a second class citizen which I now felt I had become. In the end I went with him.

Milton, East Knoyle

We soon found a small cottage to rent. It was in the village of Milton, near East Knoyle in Wiltshire. It suited Dolly very nicely as Janice, Richard and Caroline, who was two months younger than Simon, lived about 100 yards away. The cottage was tiny, with one small bedroom and a minute box room which Simon slept in. A very tiny sitting room/kitchen and bathroom completed the entire property. However it was the next door neighbour who made it for me. His name was Buzzy Grey and he was the local grave digger. He obviously took to me and used to arrive at the back door with bunches of flowers, usually plastic ones but occasionally fresh, and tell me in his broad Wiltshire accent, "I got these of a grave, I did." Once he came with some nice looking freshly dug potatoes. Again the accent, "These are real good potatoes. I buried my last dog in that plot." Needless to say, I couldn't bring myself to eat them!

Anton and the Ghost

It was while we were living in Wiltshire, near Mere that I learnt about Anton's first job in Estate Agency and his run in with the ghost of Staverdale Priory.

When Anton, aged seventeen, was a young negotiator with an Estate Agent in Mere he was asked to show an Elizabethan property called Staverdale Priory. The Priory had been sacked in Henry VIII's day and the monks turned out or killed.

The couple, who were interested in buying the place, arrived separately from Anton. The house was approached down a long drive and was blocked off some way from the house by large iron gates which were rusted locked. On either side of the overgrown driveway were deep ditches and beyond them high thorn hedges. Anton parked his car facing the gates, while the couple turned their car round. The three of them let themselves into the parkland through a small side gate and made their way to the old house. Anton said that all the time they walked round the ground floor the three of them kept looking over their shoulders. He asked the couple if they would like to see the upper floors. They said no, they just wanted to leave because they hated the place and felt very frightened – as though someone or something was following them. They quickly left and made their way back to the cars.

Upon arriving at their cars, the couple climbed into theirs and drove away. Anton got into his and started to turn it round. As he reversed, one of his rear wheels went slightly into the ditch. Wondering how badly it was in, Anton climbed out of his car and leant over. As he did so, something gripped him by his shoulder, lifted him completely off the ground and hurled him into the ditch which was filled with brambles and stinging nettles. Furious and fighting mad, he climbed out, and ready to thump whoever had done this to him. There was nobody on the drive and no way anyone could have escaped over or through the hedges. He rushed back inside the rusty gate to see if the person had run that way. Inside the gate it was just grassland and no shrubs or trees where someone could have hidden. Then he realised that when he and the other people walked on the drive the loose gravel had crunched under their feet, but whatever came up behind him had been absolutely silent. He got into his car and *drove* it out!

Upon arriving back at the office, his boss said, "What happened to you? You look as though you've seen a ghost!"

He refused to ever again go within ten miles of that house.

Boat Auctions

Before Anton was called up to serve in the army he had been an articled clerk with Woolley and Wallis, Estate Agents and Auctioneers, where he trained as an auctioneer. He became great friends with Tim Woolley and Andrew Lamont also articled clerks. Upon leaving the army Anton needed to find a job. He decided not to go back into Estate Agency or cattle auctioneering, but to use his skills elsewhere. He saw an advertisement for boat auctions and with his love of sailing he wrote to the company and offered his services. They accepted and Anton began developing the business at Marlow on the Thames. He was paid £5 per week!

Sean's Birth

We found a house to rent in Lodsworth, near Midhurst, in West Sussex and moved in. By this time I was pregnant with Sean, my second son. Sean was born at home on the 13th February 1965. My mother came down two weeks before Sean was arrived. I remember her anger when one evening Anton asked me to make him a cup of coffee. My mother offered to get it for him as I was very tired and was ready to go to bed. Anton turned on her and said that I was his wife and I must get it for him. She was furious.

The first warning that Sean was arriving was in the early hours of the 13th. We phoned the midwife and the doctor at about 6.30 am. My normal midwife was, unfortunately, away on holiday that week and so Mrs Russell came. Sadly for her, she was partially crippled with cerebral palsy – and she hated men. Mrs Russell arrived and put me on the 'gas and air' machine which had been delivered several days earlier. She took one look at me and announced that the baby wasn't due yet, and anyway she wasn't going to deliver any babies until she had eaten some breakfast and my mother had read her cards for her. I was left breathing in the gas and air.

The doctor came next and told Anton that we didn't take the right newspaper so he left to go and get his own. With that, Mrs Russell decided the baby should be born.

"Come on girl," she said, "Let's have that baby out before the doctor returns because if he isn't here for the birth, he won't get paid as much!" She removed the machine and told me to start pushing. However the doctor did get back in time and Sean was born at 10.45 am. Anton had been sitting on the stairs with Simon trying to make up his mind whether to come in and witness the birth. By the time he'd decided to watch, it was too late, Sean had arrived.

Next day Mrs Russell returned and proceeded to weigh Sean. "This baby has lost a 1lb," she said.

"No he hasn't," I replied.

"Yes, he has. He was eight pounds yesterday and he's only seven pounds today." she kept on insisting.

"Don't you remember?" I reminded her, "You forgot to bring your scales yesterday and so you just held him up in your hands and said, 'Oh, about eight pounds'."

Two days later she was back and began rummaging in the drawer where I kept the baby clothes, muttering as she did so, "Those who have shall give to those who have not." She removed a shawl and a few other things, all second hand because we didn't have any money to buy lots of new things. She explained that a young Catholic Irish mother had, while giving birth, haemorrhaged. Her husband called the parish priest first and then the midwife. When Mrs Russell arrived at the house the priest was administrating 'Last Rites'. The two of them argued over the bed with the priest insisting he needed to save the woman's soul and Mrs Russell telling him in no uncertain terms that if he got out of the way he wouldn't need to save her soul. The ambulance arrived to take the mother and baby to hospital. Mrs Russell went with the baby and told the priest that if he had to continue with his mumbo-jumbo, he'd better get in as well.

Upon reaching the hospital in Chichester, the nurses took the mother straight to surgery with the priest walking quickly alongside. Mrs Russell followed, carrying the newborn baby. As she passed through the waiting room full of new fathers and those waiting for their wives to give birth, she turned, stopped and looked scathingly at them. "You bloody men! Look what you bring us women to." I am pleased to say that the young mother survived and her baby soon grew out of the baby clothes Mrs Russell had pinched.

The following Sunday the priest preached against meddling women. Mrs Russell knew it was meant for her. Meeting Mrs Russell and her involvement with Sean's birth was an experience I wouldn't have missed for the world!

I look back on those days at Lodsworth with some sadness. I realised by this time that the man I was married to was virtually frigid and there was nothing I could do to change the situation. I was twenty two and, in those days, very pretty and I could not understand why he was that way.

Anton's Electrical Expertise!

We did have an amusing occasion when Anton, who at that time, I did not think, was very practical, although later he built his own airplane, decided to change a light bulb. I don't know what he did but he managed to fuse all the lights in the house. After that they were totally weird. As each of the four independent switches in the sitting room was activated the lights became dimmer and dimmer, instead of each one switching just one light on at a time. The kitchen switch suddenly only worked the outside lights and if we wanted the dining room ones on we had to go upstairs to turn on the bathroom switch. The whole system had gone completely haywire, which was what the electrician said when he came to check them out. They were still encased in the old lead wiring.

Jo at Cowdray House

It was while we were living in Lodsworth that my sister Jo went to Cowdray House to work as a nanny for the family's three youngest children. Lucy was the eldest, and then Charles and the youngest, and most intelligent, was an attractive child with huge grey eyes named Roseanna, Rosie to all of us.

Rosie came to Jo's funeral in October 2008 and told us about Jo arriving for the first time. Accompanied by mother, they arrived at the front door. Jo was wearing her trendy Mary Quant clothes, a miniskirt and huge false eyelashes covered with masses of jet black mascara. She was also very nervous.

She had only been at Cowdray for a couple of weeks when Rosie went down with a very serious viral illness. She was running a temperature of 105. Jo was only nineteen at the time and was naturally very frightened. Although she tried hard to persuade Rosie's mother, Lady Cowdray, to return from London, she was forced to nurse Rosie by herself. It was only when Rosie was on the road to recovery that Lady Cowdray returned.

Rosie was about four when I began visiting Cowdray with Simon and Sean. My children loved the nursery where all the children's toys were kept. I can remember taking them to one of Rosie's birthday parties and was appalled to find all these small children sitting down to tea with Crown Derby china set out for them to eat off. When I remonstrated with Jo she told me that Lord Cowdray owned the Crown Derby works and the plates could be replaced.

It was at this birthday party that we were introduced to a Punch and Judy Show. The children loved it and I was green with envy because there was no way I could afford to hire the entertainer and so, a couple of years later, I made my own theatre and puppets out of papier mache. Unable to afford to buy enough plasticine, to model the heads, I used a raw potato which I then covered with plasticine and then small scraps of paper held together with home made cooked flour and water paste. I then had to cut open the heads to remove the potato and plasticine to make the next one.

I also wrote the script and made a portable puppet theatre and did the shows myself. The 'sausages' were made out of pink fabric stuffed with cotton wool. I had them for years even taking them to the United States, where they were partly destroyed by our lovely dog who couldn't resist chewing them, and then years later, I made a new set to entertain the grandchildren. They are still enjoyed by the Women's Institute ladies when I am invited to go and do talks.

One of Charles's school friends from Harrow who really impressed three year old Simon was a large black boy called Jigme. He was always smiling and laughing and talking about his home in Bhutan, where he is now King.

After about two years my sister Jo decided she wanted to go back to live in London and because mother had sold her house near Battle and hadn't found a suitable alternative, she applied for Jo's job. After all, she said, it would make a nice change to have a comfortable house to live in *and* get paid for it. She was accepted and remained there until Rosie was sent off to boarding school. Rosie has always said that my mother was the greatest influence in her life.

Two things occurred while mother was there. One day a young man from Sotheby's arrived to do a valuation. He told mother about his visit to an old lady on his way to Cowdray She had produced a picture by Whistler and he was sure it was an original. Mother explained that it couldn't be because the original was hanging in a dark passage at Cowdray, put there because nobody liked it. She was right and the young man was forced to tell the old lady the bad news.

Another time, when Charles was home from school with a broken leg, Mother was pushing his wheel chair through the main hall when she saw one of the housemaids ascending the staircase. Remembering she wanted to speak to Alison, she called out her name. Alison completely ignored her and continued up the stairs and into Lady Cowdray's bedroom. Feeling a bit irritated Mother questioned Alison's presence in that part of the house. Then she recalled that Alison always wore very short skirts and the maid she had followed had a skirt down to her ankles. All this happened in broad daylight. Later she asked Lord Cowdray about the ghost and he told her that a maid had thrown herself out of the window of the bedroom in about 1907.

The Cowdrays were very kind to her and she enjoyed her time there. Some of the guests thought it was rather odd because she was the nanny and yet she had grown up with people like the Duke of Athol who came down to visit and enjoyed talks with her about former mutual friends.

Birdham, Near Chichester

Before Mother went to Cowdray Park we had moved again. This time it was to live on a houseboat on the Birdham canal. Anton left his job the boat auction firm when it went bust and he joined Salterns Yacht Agency at Birdham Pool, alongside the new Chichester Yacht Basin, which was then in the process of being constructed. Again I look back and think of the stupidity of living on a small houseboat with a toddler and a baby but Anton as usual was insistent.

Ffolletts (1967)

It was not long before we left there and moved into a house called 'Ffolletts'. Soon after we went to Ffolletts, Sean, aged thirteen months got out of his cot three days running. When I questioned Simon, who was nearly three, he said, "He fly like a helicopter." In other words, he'd climbed up the cot rails and thrown himself on to the floor. We switched him to a proper bed immediately.

It was also in Birdham and, because it was expensive to rent, my mother moved in followed by David Smithells, who was a workmate of Anton's. Mother took over looking after Simon and Sean and so I was able to get a job, which I did at the Yacht Agency as a typist/telephonist. I was twenty-four by now and had already been a hotel receptionist, travel agent, watch salesperson and was now a clerical worker.

While I was at work one day and Mother was looking after Simon and Sean, she heard the sound of water running and Simon saying, "Come on Seanie, come on, we've got to put the fire out." To her horror she discovered my two sons dragging a hose up the stairs and water pouring down into the hall. Dressed in their little black shiny mackintoshes with matching sou'wester hats they were playing at being firemen.

I celebrated my twenty-fifth birthday at Ffolletts and it was probably the worst one I've had. The weather was awful, we were broke, I had two small children, I couldn't drive and one of the girls who had sailed out to Hong Kong with me, Carole Goldie, came down to visit us in her smart little sports car! I remember thinking that I was a *quarter of a century old* and felt very miserable.

When I think of the mothers nowadays I look back to doing my weekly shop in Chichester. I would take the large pram with Simon and Sean in it as far as the bus stop and then leave it behind the hedge. Then we would catch the bus into the town. With arms loaded down with groceries and two small boys to manage, I struggled back to the bus and the pram to return home. It was hard work!

I did eventually learn to drive and after three failures managed to pass my test. I had been driving one month when Anton decided it might be a good idea to change cars again. This time he'd been offered a great car, he said. It was a two-seater Aston Martin which the owner agreed we could have for £200! When I pointed out that it wasn't really suitable with two children and I'd only been driving one month, he reluctantly turned it down.

Itchenor, 1968

We found a house to buy and were on the move again. This time it was an unfinished modern house which came on the market when the builder went bankrupt. It was at the end of a road with fields beyond, and the sitting room faced due west so we called it Sundown. Having found someone to finish the electrical side of things, Anton decided, that in order to save money, I should do the painting. It was bare wood, with quite a lot of boards on the outside of the house as well as in. I began with the knotting, priming and undercoating before getting down to the top coat of gloss paint. It took ages!

At the end of the garden, which was completely overgrown, was a huge bramble bush. I could see there were trees underneath its twenty foot height because the odd branch stuck out and that was another of my jobs. I began to cut and drag the huge long, tangled, prickly strands of bramble off and eventually uncovered not one tree but *four!*

Anton offered to rotovate the garden and it was during this occupation that he dug up a World War II bottle bomb. I was out and so he loaded the children and the unexploded bomb into the car and drove to the nearest police station. They were appalled when he walked in and placed it on their front desk and even more appalled when they realised he'd brought his two small sons with him.

While living at Sundown, Simon and Sean attended the local nursery school. It didn't matter what clothes I put Sean into to go to school because he would always change into one of his 'costumes'. It might be his cowboy suit, but more often it was the guardsman's uniform, which had once been a pageboy's outfit and graced a society wedding. It consisted of white satin knee britches, a red jacket and a fur bearskin, to which he added his father's brown leather army 'Sans Browne'. On an occasion when I was talking to one of his teachers, she told me that while the other children had their morning milk, Sean insisted on drinking coffee with the staff!

I got my first washing machine! Can you imagine having been married nearly six years and having two children now aged five and four, that I had been forced to wash everything by hand? It was a washer/dryer and I loved it, but before I could get too attached to the luxury, Anton had accepted an offer from John and Whit Newton, the American owners of American Marine, based in Hong Kong, to become their sales manager for Europe and everywhere else outside the United States, and we were planning our next move, this time to California.

CHAPTER 12
LAGUNA NIGUEL - 1969

Our Move the States

Anton departed ahead of us to sort out accommodation, while I let the house and went to East Sussex to stay for a couple of weeks with Jenny and Roger Farrant. Jenny had married Roger while I was away in Hong Kong. Poor Jenny and Roger tried so hard to have children. I believe she miscarried at least seven times before accepting her fate and adopting Paul, now a lovely young man.

They were living in a modern farm cottage in Northiam. Soon after that they moved into Great Knelle, a large farmhouse in Beckley just outside Northiam. Jenny and I really laughed when we went to look at it. There was only one lavatory in the building, which had six or seven bedrooms, and it was at the end of a long corridor connecting the rooms upstairs. The loo must have been nearly fifteen feet long with the toilet bowl at the far end and the loo roll hung on the back of the door - as far away as you could possibly get!

Northiam was a strange village; mother always said that the whole village was haunted. It was certainly filled with unusual people, Jenny included!

Arriving in California

Simon, Sean and I flew out to California in early May. Simon was not quite six and Sean had his fourth birthday before we left. I had made myself a very classy black and white outfit, which was Dior design and changed into it before we got off the plane.

Anton met us, driving a green Pontiac and drove us to the house he had bought in Laguna Niguel. The address was 23312 Telfair Drive and it was on a corner plot with magnificent views over Crown Valley which was almost completely unspoilt in those days. The house was single story and Anton had furnished it for us although the garden was completely bare with dreadful soil because the contractors had simply taken the top off the hill. It took a lot of digging manure into it to get anything to grow.

He also introduced us to Moi Moi, a lovely puppy, whose mother was a thoroughbred long nosed collie. We were not sure about Moi Moi's father but he could have been a German shepherd because, although Moi Moi had his mother's colouring, he had a much shorter, fatter nose. In fact he looked exactly like a lion with a huge golden mane. He became a great favourite in the neighbourhood and on several occasions people called him into their houses to save him from the Dog Pound Patrol. It was illegal to allow your dog to run loose.

Anton showed us the incredible view and explained that there was a five thousand foot mountain about twenty miles away which we would normally be able to see, but it was nearly a month before we believed him. Later we realised that the mist rolls in from the sea in May and completely obscures the distance. Then on June 1st I woke up to find the Saddleback Mountain looking so clear you could almost make out individual bushes and trees. It was amazing.

Crown Valley Highlands

Everyone in the development was new to the area. Our neighbours consisted of Scots, Greeks, a large plump, part Japanese, part Hawaiian man married to a cute blond cheer leader type of girl, and people from all over the United States – New England, Texas, Arizona, Illinois and elsewhere. The Americans ranged from attorneys, company directors to electricians and construction workers – all receiving roughly the same amount of pay during the building boom in Orange County. Because nobody knew anyone, we all got together very quickly, usually meeting down at the private swimming pool. I remember when Sally

Williams, who lived round the corner with Richard her husband and their three children, arrived and proceeded to bring everyone together on Independence Day on July 4th for a party. From then on we got to know so many people. One American asked me if we celebrated Independence Day in England. "No," I replied cynically, "We lost the war!" However we joined in the fun anyway.

Sally became my best friend and without too much difficulty I might add, encouraged me to become extremely lazy. As soon as our husbands left for work we would wander round, usually in bare feet, to one or the other's house to drink endless cups of coffee and to watch soap stories on television. My house was untidy, but Sally's was beyond belief. I don't think she ever put anything away and often the breakfast cereal, which was usually scattered all over her kitchen table and floor, would still be there when she was preparing supper. Occasionally we would swap houses to clean each others. It was a nightmare to do Sally's.

Other friends were Annabel, the very intense wife of a medical litigation attorney, and Frances who was quite laid back. Frances had two sons Mikey and Terry. Sally and I were convinced that Terry would turn out to be psychopath as at the age of three he was already showing signs of cruelty to animals.

We hadn't been living in our new house long when I noticed Frances running out of her house screaming, followed by a group of small boys, my two included, with a large snake being carried by Mark, Sally's eldest.

I heard them say, "Come on Simon, let's go and get your mom!" Now I am not very fond of snakes but I knew that if I showed any fear, as Frances had done, they would plague me for life. Simon came rushing into the house with the other boys and Mark, who had the snake hidden behind his back.

"We've got something to show you." Simon said.

"Oh have you?" I replied as they exposed the snake and waited for me to scream.

"Would you like to hold it?"

"OK," said I trying not to let it show that I was terrified.

"Can we put it round you neck?"

"OK." I said again. Then after a moment of two they removed the snake and said, "Come on Simon, your mom's no fun, let's go and get Tom's mom." They never bothered to tease me with snakes again.

Because the builders had built the new estate on virgin hillsides there were many wild animals. The snake the children had tried to scare me with was a California King snake, but there were also the harmless Gopher snakes and the deadly Rattle snakes. Other creatures included opossums, skunks, and vultures with bare red necks. The smell of a skunk is almost indescribable, especially on the two occasions when Moi Moi was sprayed upon and rushed into the house. I learnt very quickly that the only way to get rid of the stench on the dog's fur is to douse it in, of all things, tomato juice. Whoever discovered this must have been weird! With a dog the size of ours it took quite a lot of very large tins of tomato juice. We had to put him in the bath and tip the juice all over him. With the smell so strong it was pretty horrible.

Over the months Sally, Frances and I worked on our back gardens, or yards as we called them. We rented a cultivator to dig the ground over. I was the strongest and did the lion's share of the work. I even built a concrete pond with a working mini waterfall. The only trouble was that I didn't mix and pour all the concrete on the same day and so where one lot had set there was always a leak which meant we had to keep topping it up.

Simon's Pets

Simon began his collection of pets. Along with the dog, we bought some black and white rats. Unfortunately we thought they were both male until the first litter of baby rats turned up. Simon thought he was on to a good thing when he found he could sell the babies back to the pet shop, but that came to a grinding halt when he discovered that these cute little creatures were sold on as live bait for snakes!

Then he came home with his first iguana. Although he only had one while we lived in the States, he has had several later on in his life. There were also terrapins, snakes he found in the hills and brought home, baby alligators and finally a tarantula, which he'd also caught in the wild. It was the snakes I objected to, at least it was when they went missing in the house. After the third one vanished I forbade him to bring home any more so he went out and caught a tarantula which lived in a glass tank and fed it live crickets. It didn't remain with us long because it ate the crickets at night and Simon objected to be woken up when the crunching of the back legs became too loud! Actually, although I wasn't keen on touching it, Simon allowed it to walk slowly up his bare arm. I was not terrified by it but Anton was. When we moved back to England Simon acquired yet another pet, this time a ferret! Later in life he had iguanas and still has a snake and his daughter Melzie a lizard.

Our Neighbours

It was 1969 – the height of flower power and songs about San Francisco, so it wasn't surprising that three of our immediate neighbours were quiet, peaceful and mostly *stoned* hippies.

Fred had long blonde hair and a beard; Gary, a pseudo Reverend, (he had bought the title to avoid Vietnam) and Jennifer, a totally beautiful, full-blooded Cherokee Indian. Fred never seemed to do any work, except during the Art Festival in Laguna Beach where he and Jennifer had a booth. She painted stones, this lovely girl with jet-black hair that hung way down past her waist. Gary worked, I'm not sure what at, but it was probably something where he could dodge anyone who might have suggested he should be fighting with the American Marines. I don't quite know what the relationship was between these three. Sally drifted off one summer in a Volkswagen bus with her three children and Fred and spent a couple of months living beside a river in northern California with other peaceful people, while Gary and Jennifer just seemed to disappear.

Parties in the Highlands

The parties in Crown Valley Highlands were crazy in the early seventies. People indulged in drugs, drinking and sex. California was very open and liberal in those days before the onset of HIV. Actually I didn't get involved in the drugs scene, I was much too afraid of being deported as we were still thought of as visitors to the United States. However the 'Annie Greensprings Blackberry Wine' went down quite well, especially when mixed with vodka. When the marijuana and LSD came out I crept away.

Anton did succumb accidentally on one occasion. Fred and friends invited all the neighbours to 'come on over', and bring what ever stimulant we wanted. We took wine and beer. During the evening many of the group were sitting round in a circle. I don't smoke, and have never done after watching my father cough and choke with emphysema, and so I wasn't involved. Fred lit a handmade 'cigarette', clipped it into a pair of tweezers and passed it to Anton who looked at it and thought, how sad that they can't afford proper cigarettes and have to roll their own. He then puffed away at it while Fred and the others sat and watched and waited for him to pass it round the circle. Suddenly, realising they were all looking at him, Anton pulled out his pack of Marlboros, offered the open packet and said, "Oh, sorry! Would you like a cigarette?"

On another occasion, Frances's husband Gary came over and asked if I would like to join them, and a few close friends, for a 'party' in his garage that evening. He warned me not tell anyone. About 8.00pm I went, looking over my shoulder in case any cops were around. Boy, was I naïve! We made sure our children were asleep and then in total darkness Gary ran the 'film'. The first 'blue' film I had ever seen. I do not remember very much about it except screaming with laughter because the male character took off everything except his flat cap and socks.

A different evening saw eight of us, only Sally and Richard were married to each other while the rest of us had spouses. Anton was away on business while two other men, including the home owner, were separated and had girlfriends in attendance and one other man who preferred to leave his wife at home. We met at the house next door to Sally's. In those days I was still wearing glasses, which I hated, and so I took them off and left them on a table near the front door. For some reason I was feeling very miserable that evening and sat on the floor talking to Richard, a kindly alcoholic. While he was trying to cheer me up, and with tears trickling down my cheeks, I vaguely heard someone say, 'let's take it all off'. It was about half an hour later, when I looked over my shoulder, I saw through a haze of sweet smelling smoke that Richard and I were the only ones with any clothes on. Not into drugs I panicked and decided it was time to depart.

I couldn't reach my glasses without it being obvious, and so I crawled across the living room floor behind the furniture, then the kitchen, quietly opened the back door and ran home. Next day, when I went back to retrieve my specs, I discovered I was very unpopular for leaving. The numbers were wrong. High on a combination of LSD and marijuana four men and three women who all ended up on the same king sized waterbed at the same time! Whatever they were on that evening was definitely something the cops would have busted them for. At the time I was relieved I had chickened out but now, after nearly forty years, I look back and think *damn* - what did I miss!.

We didn't just party at home – the wives would go off in a group to the nightspots of Laguna Beach and drink and dance the night away. We all wore mini skirts or hot pants. I had a pair of very soft leather hot pants, which were really fun to dance in. Sally and I also had tiny white crocheted mini dresses which scarcely covered our knickers. It was a fine art bending down to pick anything up.

The Ouija Board

One evening one of our other close neighbours came over to ask me to go to their house. Her father-in-law had died of a heart attack that day back in New York. Dorothy told me her husband Roy was distraught as he hadn't been able to say good bye to his father. He was sure his father would have given him a message. Did I think I could get through using the ouija board? I agreed to go to their house where we laid out the letters of the alphabet in a circle and placed an upside down glass in the middle. With the three of us putting one finger on the top of the glass it began to move almost immediately. The first words spelt out were shocking swear words and Dorothy immediately said that although she'd put up with *her* father swearing at her while he was alive, she was damned if she accept it now. With that she went to bed and so it left Roy and me. The glass began to spell out absolute nonsense and I realised Roy had taken his finger off and was sitting with his head in his hands, crying.

"I'm sorry Roy; nothing is coming through, just rubbish."

"You've forgotten," he replied, "I am Czechoslovakian. That is Czech that is coming though and one of the words spelt out was my father's pet name for my mother!"

The Flying Club

In the time between Anton leaving England and Simon, Sean and I arriving in southern California, Anton had discovered how inexpensive it was to learn to fly and as it was one of his blinding ambitions, because his father had flown Spitfires, he enrolled in flying lessons at San Juan Capistrano Airfield. It was an amazing little airport. Seventeen hundred feet of a dirt landing strip. On one side stood the tiny clubhouse and a number of airplanes and on the other a wide, deep storm channel to carry flood waters out to the sea. The area opposite the little airport was still undeveloped when I took my first flying lessons.

Anton went solo in about five hours. He had eaten, slept, dreamt how to fly and was a natural. I took longer, but still went solo at just over ten hours flying time. Looking back on it, I wasn't ready. I did manage to get the airplane down on the second attempt after my instructor, John, jumped out and sent me off. I can still recall the moment. John climbed out of the cockpit and said, "Off you go," and I did. It was only when I was airborne that I thought, oh my God! – I couldn't just pull over to the side of the road to think about it, I was up there, on my own and had to land the two-seater airplane. The first approach was too low, I added power and I went round again. The next time I landed so heavily the airplane bounced a couple of times before staying down and when it stopped I didn't even know how to switch the engine off.

Climbing out of the cockpit I found that I had hit the ground so hard the catches on the engine cowling had all come undone! We laughed about it later when they cut off part of the back of my shirt to put up on the wall of the clubhouse as proof that I had 'gone solo'. I did another ten hours flying, sometimes with the instructor and sometimes solo, and then gave it up. I really hated learning to 'stall' the plane and to do tight turns, one wing down, round a point on the ground. I think stalling was the worst, when I had to pull back on the controls and force the nose of the plane up and up until, shuddering, the whole aircraft fell away, nose down until I had to pull it out and it began to fly again. I hate roller coasters and so I was never going to enjoy this part of flying, straight and level was OK but not the manoeuvres we had to learn in order to deal with emergencies. However I knew that I could land a plane if it ever became necessary.

Landing on the Private Airstrip

Anton passed his private pilot's license very quickly and enjoyed hiring one of the club planes. One afternoon he took me flying and decided to land on a private dirt air strip miles from anywhere - we thought. He wanted a cigarette and insisted on landing. I was not very happy as I hate the idea of breaking the law.

"Nonsense," said Anton, "nobody will know. We're only going to be here for a few minutes." However, unseen by us, a Sheriff's car was heading straight towards the plane. He screeched to a halt and parked right up against the front of the plane so we couldn't fly away.

"Where are you from?" he asked in an aggressive tone.

"Southampton, England. Where are we?" Anton replied.

"You got any ID?" The only ID we had on us was an English Barclaycard and I don't remember why we had that.

By this time the cop had us spread eagled up against the side of the plane. It turned out that we were only about thirty miles from the Mexican border and we could have had anything on board, including illegal immigrants.

"Where are the documents for the plane?" Anton lied and said he had left them at the clubhouse along with his personal ID etc.

By this time the cop was banging on the wings of the airplane.

"What are you looking for?" asked Anton thinking it was drugs, but they wouldn't make a noise.

The cop had mellowed a little and told us he was checking to see if we were illegally importing parakeets.

Of course Anton had to make a joke and say that if they flapped hard enough we didn't need to start the engine!

The cop then told us to fly straight back to the airfield and he would follow us in his car. As soon as we took off I reminded Anton he'd left his wallet at home. Flying as fast as the plane would go; Anton skipped the approach routine and flew straight in. While he shut down the engine, I ran into the clubhouse to phone our next door neighbour and ask him to break into the house and then dash down before the cop could reach the airport. Unfortunately the cop got there first, but all the members kept him talking. Eventually Roy, our neighbour turned up.

The cop looked at Anton and said, "When I was in the Civil Air Patrol we were always landing in illegal places, but the difference was son, I didn't get caught!"

Building the Volkesplane

Soon after this, Anton knew he wanted his own plane and so he decided to build one. He bought the plans to the 'Volkesplane'. The designer was the man who had designed the Convair 880. It certainly wasn't a pretty plane but it was immensely strong as Anton was to prove later after he crash landed it in a canyon.

We had a three car garage at Telfair Drive in Crown Valley Highlands. Anton assembled tools, wood and the appropriate equipment to build his plane. Whilst working on it Simon, who was fascinated by the project, managed to persuade his father not to make *fatal mistake*. Anton had built the fuselage and one wing and began jigging up for the second. Of course the plans only showed the one wing and Anton was about to duplicate it! Simon, who was only about seven or eight at the time was watching his father who was about to glue the second wing.

"Dad, dad!" he shouted, only to be told by his father to shut up. "But dad if you do it that way you will have two left wings!"

He was right and Anton had to re-jig the whole frame. Apart from almost making mistakes the other thing we had to watch out for were the Black Widow spiders. They had an evil habit of hiding in dark corners in the garage and could give a pretty nasty, if not fatal bite.

When it was eventually built, which was after we moved *again* - to Mission Viejo this time, he painted it in British RAF naval colours. OK in California, but not so good in England when he brought it back here several years later. It had a dark blue top to the fuselage and light blue below. RAF roundels and black and white stripes on the wings completed the paintwork. Anton chose these colours because there were a number of American 'War Birds' (airplanes) based at the airport and he wanted to compete with them.

Run In's with the Cops

Both Anton and I had incidents with the police. I remember the first time I was stopped; it was in the middle of Laguna Beach. We had bought a Datsun pick-up truck from a fellow employee of American Marine, the company Anton was working for. Carl sold us this vehicle but failed to point out that it hadn't been registered for that year. I was very surprised when the cop pulled me over.

"What have I done wrong?" I asked.

"You haven't registered your vehicle, ma'am," he said.

"How do you know?" I asked innocently.

"The small sticker on your rear number plate is out of date."

"Could you show me where it is supposed to be?"

He pointed it out explaining that it was six months out of date. I told him we had only just bought the truck, but he said he'd have to give me a ticket anyway.

"Can I see your vehicle documents, please?"

"If you tell me what they look like and where I might find them, I'll be happy to show you."

"Most folks keep them in the glove compartment." But of course

133

they weren't there. So much for buying things from so called friends! I really wasn't trying to be funny; I did not know what he was talking about. I think we had only been in the States for a couple of months when this happened.

While the cop was writing out the ticket, I wondered what one was supposed to talk about. I had just seen an article in the newspaper that day about a policeman who had been shouted at by a rude motorist who happened to be driving past when the cop was issuing a ticket to another motorist. The driver yelled that he was a pig. The man was caught and told by the judge he could either spend a month in jail, or pay $200 and sit in a pig pen for a day. I told this story to the cop and added that my sympathies were with the pigs! My friendly cop promptly tore up the ticket and asked me which paper I'd read it in.

Anton's experience occurred when he was driving home from Los Angeles airport after a business trip. Because it was late evening and we lived about an hour and a half away, he hired a car from Avis. Heading south on the San Diego Freeway he became aware of flashing lights. Knowing that he had been speeding, he immediately pulled over, not on to the hard shoulder but into the centre divider. The Highway patrolman got out and asked him to produce his driving licence, which he did – it was an English one because after seven years he had never got round to passing the Californian test. Speaking in his most British accent, he really laid it on thick; he asked the cop what he had done wrong. Speeding was the answer.

"Is this your car, sir?"

"No I've just hired it from Avis."

"Where are you going?"

Anton again spoke in an as upmarket British voice as he could while he pulled out his address book. "I'm heading for Laguna Niguel," (Usually pronounced with hard g's), Anton deliberately totally mispronounced the two words, "Am I going in the right direction?"

"How long are you here for?"

"Two weeks." This was true as he was off on another business trip.

"Well you drive safely sir," and the cop let him go.

The following Saturday we were at a flying club party at somebody's home and a cop car pulled up. Anton immediately called out to the driver, who was a flying friend, but on duty that night.

"Hey, Len I've got a really great story for you!"

"Hang on a minute Anton, I think my buddy in the car would like to hear this one!" and out got the same Highway Patrolman who had let Anton off scot free. Len explained he had been in the car on the night of the speeding offence and had recognised Anton and waited in the dark to see what sort of cock and bull story he would come up with. Len's buddy was not amused and just said, "The next time I stop you, I'll throw the book at you!"

Another time we were driving back from our house in June Lake. Anton was driving and, as usual, way over the limit. The road across the desert is like a switch back. I guess they just laid the tarmac over the lumps. As we hurtled south a Highway Patrolman was driving fast in the opposite direction. We both went over the same large hump and as we shot past the cop, we saw him glance across with a look of shock.

"Oh Hell," said Anton, "he'll come after us."

We decided to turn off the road as quickly as possible and so at the very first dirt road turning we spun off with dust flying everywhere. The road ended quickly and we all dived out to pretend we were having a picnic. Suddenly another car followed us and was followed by the cops. Anton really thought he had had it – but the cop ignored us and gave a ticket to the other fellow! We had to laugh because the place we had chosen for our picnic was the local rubbish tip.

Tim Hyde and the California Junior Lifeguards

Among friends and business acquaintances who came to visit us were my sister Jo, who stayed for several months and our nephew Tim, who spent a number of weeks with us one summer when he was aged about ten. I look back with shame at what we made him do. Simon and Sean were members of the California Junior Lifeguards and went down to Salt Creek, a fabulous swimming and surfing beach. The course was tough and the final test gruelling. Each child had to run a hundred yards down the beach in thick sand, then swim out round a buoy which was bobbing away about two hundred yards out and then run back down the beach again. Tim was not a good swimmer and was quite timid. He was desperate to get his red lifeguard shorts and the badge that went with them, but he was terrified. Anton insisted he went. The class were very good, they all decided to support Tim, and although they had done their tests, they insisted on doing it again with Tim.

I wrote it in the first person as Tim described his experience to me.

I sat with my head half buried in my knees watching the grey Pacific Ocean rolling in over the sands. At ten years old every wave looks gigantic like those ridden by surfers in Hawaii. I was so afraid – this was the day I had to take my Junior Lifeguard test.

I wriggled my feet deeper into the sand. Perhaps if I pushed them far enough I wouldn't be able to move. The warm sand felt gritty between my toes. A few inches below the surface my feet reached the cold damp beach that hadn't been warmed and dried by the sun. I pushed my feet harder but the sand was too solid.

WHY were my aunt and uncle making me do this Lifeguard course? They signed me up, along with my cousins Simon and Sean, for two weeks of my holiday in California. My aunt Anna had promised to buy me a grown up fishing rod if I passed. I really wanted the rod but I thought I was too scared.

I looked round at the other boys and girls – I was pale compared with their sun bronzed bodies. Everybody else had completed the test and now it was my turn.

"Come on Tim, you can do it!"

No I can't! I CAN'T! I screamed in my mind. Sean dragged me to my feet. He and Simon said they would come with me. I had to run one hundred yards up the beach and back again before plunging into that ghastly build up of waves. I managed to make my way along the beach, going as slowly as I could just to put off the terrifying ordeal ahead.

My knees kept buckling under me and I tripped and fell over once, winding myself. Fighting back the tears, my worst nightmare faced me – I had to swim out round a buoy and back again. The waves seemed huge.

I waded out as far a possible and found the whole class coming with me, including the instructors. Someone might rescue me before I disappeared forever beneath the cold forbidding ocean.

Every stroke was frightening. The buoy was so far out – two hundred yards at least! Waves splashed in my face and the buoy was as far away as ever. With my cousins and everybody else encouraging me, I kept on going.

"Come on Tim, you're nearly there", kept ringing in my ears."

*Choking and crying, salt burning my eyes, arms and legs so tired, I didn't think I could make it. I reached the surf line and tumbled round and round and upside down. Just as I thought I really **was** drowning two hands grabbed my arms and pulled me up to the surface. Suddenly my feet touched the wet sand beneath the surf and I staggered ashore and collapsed.*

I had only one hundred yards to run up and down the beach again. I reached the end and fell once more, feeling the tears drip into the dry sand beneath my face. Pain, fear, relief and a blissful feeling of success flooded my body. 'I'd done it!' I dragged myself to my knees to find the whole class surrounding me.

"Hey Tim, you were really great!" Smiling at them through my tears I saw my aunt holding out her arms to me.

"Well done Tim – I KNEW you'd make it. You are now officially a California Junior Lifeguard – and your fishing rod is in the car."

Sunlight suddenly seemed to sparkle on the tops of the waves and everything was warm with a light breeze brushing my body. I turned and ran joyfully back into the surf of the Pacific Ocean to join all the other Junior Lifeguards.

He passed and was so happy when I sewed his badge on to the swim trunks. He says now that he only did it because there were some beautiful bronzed Californian girls there and he didn't want to fail in front of them!

The next day we left for June Lake where Tim put his new fishing rod to work.

A feeling of shame

There was one occasion about which I still cringe. My mother had been out to stay during the first year of our living in southern California and was planning to visit us again. Everything was arranged at her end, flights paid and plans made. I was a coward and put off telling Anton until about two weeks before she came. He just told me to phone her and cancel it. He would not let her come! It was awful! I still feel hot and cold when I think of the unkindness and my lack of courage and determination to insist that she came. I can still hear her shock and unhappiness at my message.

Elementary School

Sitting around drinking coffee with Sally and Frances was now really boring so Sally and I became very involved with the village school when we both joined the PTA. Not being involved with committees, we arrived in our mini skirts and bare feet. We usually went around in bare feet at that time. The other ladies stared at us as we arrived because they were almost formally dressed. However we worked hard and eventually gained their respect.

Halloween Fair

We organised the summer fete and the Halloween fair. Looking back I am sure a lot of children had nightmares after going through the Haunted House. We made them crawl through a box hung with things that felt like spiders webs, put their hands into bowls with peeled grapes, which we told them were eyeballs, and cold cooked spaghetti - pigs entrails. We had ghosts that jumped out at them, but the worst sight that met them was a reconstruction of St John's head on the platter. Sitting in a cardboard box, with only his head stuck out, was one the 6th graders. I covered the box with a white sheet with a hole in the middle and then arranged a 'silver platter', again with a hole in it, round the boy's head. This we covered with fake blood and as people went past, this awful child twisted his head towards them and let out ghastly groans.

Puppets

I did a lot helping with the drama classes, including writing a play about Richard Henry Dana, the seaman who fought to improve conditions on board ship. It began as a serious play and ended in pure farce. The kids loved it.

I also assisted the 'mentally gifted' children with making papier mache puppets. We did a play about the Pilgrim Fathers arriving in the United States. Some of the children made Pilgrim Fathers and Mothers puppets, while the others concentrated on the Red Indians. During the first production we really made the audience laugh when one of the children, who had a Red Indian puppet, turned to his Red Indian son and ad libbed, "Ha, I spy the Mayflower on the horizon. Go catch me that turkey and we will scalp him and pluck him and put him in the refrigerator!"

During another performance one of the Pilgrim Father's, who was being very realistically sick over the side of the cardboard cut out Mayflower, suddenly lost first his hat and then his head. Completely undaunted the owner of this puppet proceeded to reach through the scenery to recover the parts. The play continued around her! I thought the audience would die laughing!

Cub Scouts

I became very involved with the Cub Scouts. We were Den 7 of Pack 707 and I managed to get a giant plastic blow up Seven-up bottle, which we dressed in Cub uniform. It was about six feet tall. (In the States each Den met once a week with the whole Pack only getting together once a month.) We certainly had the wildest time, but whether the boys ever learnt anything I am not sure. One afternoon we made cup cakes, which the boys iced. I gave each of them a bowl of icing and a variety of colours, cocoa and bits and pieces to decorate the tops. Most boys mixed one colour and so we had blue or red or yellow, but one kid, who was a little devil decided to put all the colours, plus the cocoa into his icing. The colour he produced was disgusting to look at. Judging, probably rightly, he made the decision that his mother wouldn't want to eat this half a dozen – so we shared them out and ate them ourselves. The first boy who grinned got a shriek of laughter; his teeth had turned a horrible shade of blue/brown. Then we all laughed because we all had the same coloured teeth.

One of the boys favourite games was hockey played with rolled up newspaper sticks. We always ended up with torn up paper all over the garden as the 'sticks' disintegrated. The other game they loved was when I pinned four sheets together, threw all their shoes underneath and on the shout of 'go' they all dived under to retrieve and put them on. They thought it was exquisitely funny when our dog jumped on top and nibbled them through the sheets.

Simon went on into the Boy Scouts and nearly achieved his Eagle badge, one of the highest awards possible. Unfortunately his peer group began making fun of him and he gave it up.

Various Jobs I Had

My first job was in Valentine Real Estate. I answered the phone and did a bit of typing. I was not allowed to sell houses or even take people out to see them, because I was not a qualified Realtor. Unlike England, you have to have taken exams before you are even allowed to do viewings.

Mr Valentine, the owner, was very proud of his name. One of my jobs was to cut the photographs into heart shapes and attached them to red backing paper! He also liked to change his windows every month and my role was to introduce a different theme. One month was Hollywood with the house photographs attached to large pretend strips of film.

He was very, very Republican, while everyone else in the office voted for the Democrats. I recall that he insisted that every letter sent out from the firm should have a note at the bottom saying –'Vote Nixon for President'. It did not go down well with the Democratic staff.

After the Real Estate work, I moved next door to the Penguin Café, where I waitressed and was a part time 'short order' cook. In other words I made hamburgers and chilli etc. The café was mostly used by the city workmen – refuse cleaners, telephone men and others, so Sally, who worked with me, and I had a great time. The café opened at 6.00am to serve breakfasts and closed at 3.00pm. The juke box ran non-stop. So many songs take me straight back there, especially American Pie.

Sally and I occasionally did other part-time jobs, although I never worked, as she did, in the topless bikini bar. We did work together one evening when we were asked to stand in for some security guards patrolling the Art Festival in Laguna Beach. We were given uniforms for the night and unloaded guns in holsters just to deter would be thieves. Sadly nobody tried to pinch anything the evening we were on duty and so it did get a bit boring. It would have been much more fun to have patrolled the 'Saw Dust' Festival across the road. Really strange people hung out there and I'm sure you could get high just walking round it from the fumes of the illegal cigarettes which filled the air. The 'Saw Dust' Festival was an unofficial offshoot of the main art festival and was named 'Saw Dust' because that was what was scattered on the ground round the stalls. So many original ideas found light of day in this funky place.

I later got a job in banking, but that was after we moved to Mission Viejo.

June Lake

Anton was doing very well with American Marine, selling lots of the Grand Banks, heavy displacement, ocean-going motor cruisers. They were not designed to travel extremely fast but were very comfortable and reliable.

It was at this time we decided to buy a cabin in the Sierra Nevadas at a lovely little town called June Lake. The drive up to this mountain retreat was amazing. Leaving the Los Angles conurbation, we travelled through the Mojave Desert, passing wonderful unspoilt towns like Johannesburg and Red Mountain which still have the old wooden sidewalks and square fronted Wild West type buildings. People continue to live there, unlike the ghost town of Bodie much further north beyond the June Lake 'turn-off'. They were all old gold mining towns, but Bodie had been a very rich source for many years until the gold ran out. At one time, it was said, there were possibly as many as 100,000 people living there and killings every day. It is still worth the effort to go and see Bodie. The houses and shops that have survived are still there as though the owners had just walked out. Cars lie rusting amongst the tumbleweed. Books remain on school desks.

Leaving the desert and heading up the eastern side of the mountains, which rise up to 14,000 feet, we passed through other wonderfully named little towns such as Independence and Lone Pine before reaching Bishop and beginning the long climb up past Mammoth Lakes, a huge winter skiing area, and on to the June Lake Loop turn off.

About half a mile after turning off to the town, there is a road sign saying 'Oh! Ridge'. On the first occasion we wondered why it should have such an odd name, however on passing the sign we went over the top of the ridge and saw the first of the series of lakes that make up the June Lake area. The lake itself was spread out before us, very deep and of a dark blue colour reflecting the sky. All round the lake Aspen trees fluttered their golden leaves, making a soft swishing sound as the wind rustled through them. We all, in unison, with the road sign said, "Oh!" Thus the name, 'Oh! Ridge'.

The house we bought was a small 'A' frame, wooden building not far beyond the ski lift area. In winter we enjoyed the skiing and in summer the fishing. The streams were packed with brown and rainbow trout. An old waiter told us that he preferred to watch the fish rather than catch them. He had a boat with a glass panel in the bottom. He told us that deep in the lake were brown trout weighing up to 60 lbs. The reason they were rarely caught was because of the way they feed with their huge mouths sucking food from the bottom while their bodies stuck straight up. It was only when they had filled their mouths they flattened out and so if they picked up your hook while feeding it was likely just to slide out again.

Three fish at once

One afternoon when Simon, who really enjoyed fishing, was sitting beside a stream with his father, Sean and I went off to do some shopping. Upon returning Sean decided to fish as well. It took me some time to untangle his rod and line. Simon was very proud that he had caught three fish. Sean strolled over to the stream and cast his line into it. He immediately, within ten seconds, hooked a nice little rainbow trout, and as he reeled it in his line caught on another loose piece line which had been abandoned in the water. This line had two hooks still attached to it and as he dragged it out along with his fish, two other fish grabbed the free hooks and he landed three fish all at one time! With that he gave up fishing for the day and annoyed Simon very much indeed by saying that fishing was really easy and he'd caught as many as his brother. Poor Simon had been there for hours!

Jenny Farrant came out to stay with us bringing her baby, Paul, with her. I finally learnt to ski on this holiday. Skiing was never my favourite sport and I hated the moguls. There was one stretch near the top of the mountain where you couldn't avoid them and I remember balancing on top of a particularly big mogul and trying to decide how to get off.

Another time, the American Marine accountant, Tony Nedderman joined us. He very nearly never made it to June Lake. Like Anton he didn't know how to obey a speed sign. Naturally, he was pulled over. Anton told him to say as little as possible, however the cop didn't appreciate his taciturnity and threatened to haul him off to the jail in Bishop.

All the way from our house in southern California to our cabin he shot a line to the children about how he had skied down Mont Blanc. They were very impressed. The following morning Tony, completely kitted out in black, and the rest of us headed for the slopes. We were a little surprised when Tony fell over twice on the way to the chair lift to take us up the mountain. Then he fell over again getting off at the top. Setting off to ski back down to the bottom, Tony took off straight towards a sheer drop of several hundred feet. Shouting at him to *'Turn, Tony'*, we then began to shout, *'Fall over, Tony!'* – He did fortunately. Simon and Sean began to laugh, but before I could send them off up the mountain to save Tony's embarrassment, he had skied straight back across the slope into a vertical wall of snow. With his nose almost touching the snow, he casually said, "I appear to be stuck." I then banished the boys and proceeded to accompany Tony back to the Ski Lodge, but not before he had fallen again, this time breaking his sun glasses and cutting his nose. It was now about 9.30 am and Tony decided that hot mulled wine was the order of the morning. He stayed there all day!

A couple of years later I found among all the papers and documents a 'Quit Claim Deed' Anton had given me to sign. It completely cut me out from the ownership of the cabin. I was naturally very angry as I had furnished the house, made all the curtains, did the cooking and cleaned it every time, especially before we left it at the end of each holiday when the others would go off for the day and leave me to clean, pack and prepare for going home. I never enjoyed going there again after the revelation. By this time we were firmly established in our next home in Mission Viejo

CHAPTER 13
MISSION VIEJO - 1974

Anton's Story of His Airplane Crash in California

(This was how Anton described the experience. I have written it as if I was telling the story).

It was an amazing little plane, not pretty but very reliable, unless of course you didn't check the petrol tank, which Anton failed to do on one occasion. The Volkesplane, being of very simple design did not have a traditional fuel gauge; it was merely a piece of bent wire stuck into a cork which floated on the surface of the petrol. When the fuel was low the length of wire got smaller, however it could get stuck and so it was necessary to visually check the contents and on this occasion it *had* stuck but Anton didn't check!

He had flown out to a 'fly-in' where pilots go to meet up with buddies from other places, at an airfield somewhere out in the desert. Having taken part in some of the demonstrations, Anton was flying home in the little 18 foot long, with a 24 foot wingspan aircraft, which looked like a giant dragonfly when viewed from the ground, suddenly, without warning the engine cut out and the propeller spun freely.

Anton's first reaction was to think, 'What the hell has happened?' Then he quickly began to look round for a place to put down. A dirt road away to the left looked promising. Banking the airplane gently he turned towards it only to notice at the last minute there were telegraph poles with electricity wires strung from them. No chance of landing there. Still wondering where he could land he surveyed the land. Crevasses criss-crossed the ground, boulders and coarse tumbleweed covered the dry earth. Anton made a hasty decision – land facing uphill. In this way the plane would stop quickly and do little damage.

The propeller had almost stopped and the open-cockpit plane was flying incredibly slowly with the ground seeming to race up at a terrifying rate. Touching down, wings brushed the tumbleweed and with wheels bounding over rocks, the airplane came to a halt just yards from hurtling into a deep crevasse. Sitting there, heart pounding while the hot mid-summer Californian breeze swept over him, Anton said his life seemed to flash past in an appalling jumble.

Startled by the sound of galloping horses' hooves, he looked up and saw a cowboy wearing a ten-gallon hat, leather chaps and a shotgun in a saddle holster.

Anton thought, have I died and gone back in time, while asking, "Who the hell are you?"

The cowboy, (a Swiss doctor out shooting coyotes, he later explained) replied in a strong foreign accent, "And who the hell are you? I ride my horse and hear a small airplane flying above me. When the engine stop, I look up and see the plane descend and hear very rude swear words coming from the sky!"

Anton, laughing in relief, asked the doctor how he could get back to civilization.

"The rancher lives that way – about two miles. You better check in with him."

After climbing out of the cockpit, Anton made his way up the steep hillside and gazed across the rough terrain towards the distant ranch house. Between him and his goal, cattle grazed peacefully. No problem there, he thought, as he strode out purposefully.

But he was wrong. As he approached the herd, a young Brahma bull emerged from the centre and stared. Anton stopped. The bull snorted and moved slightly forwards. Looking round for an escape, Anton decided to start walking again, warily watching the sturdy animal. The bull followed. Anton moved faster, the bull began to trot. Ahead of him was a deep crevasse, filled with scrubby bushes. Anton began to run – and so did the bull. Fear drove him faster – it was either the horns and being gored or reaching the crevasse.

The crevasse came first. Flinging himself over the lip, Anton rolled down the escarpment out of reach of those wicked horns. The bull stopped on the edge, snorting and pawing the ground with sharp hooves.

146

Lying there, winded and fighting for breath, he almost cried between fear and relief of escaping from the bull. It was only later that night that Anton thought about the possibility that he might have escaped one danger for another – the crevasse would surely have rattlesnakes and tarantulas as residents.

After a while Anton tentatively climbed back up and peered over the edge. It seemed that the bull had been waiting because the large beast immediately approached again.

Creeping back safety of the hollow he lay next to a bush that smelt vaguely of thyme and watched the vultures, like black silhouettes, circling lazily overhead in the sunshine. Anton wished that he was up there flying with them.

Dusk turns to night very quickly in southern California and Anton knew he should be on his way soon. The terrain was extremely rough and, in the dark, it would be easy to fall and break a leg. Gingerly edging his way towards the top of the slope again, he was relieved to see the whole herd far away on the horizon. Crossing the ground as swiftly as possible, Anton kept an eye open for the bull, always looking for an escape route if the beast should approach again.

The ranch loomed close and Anton made his way to the door to explain that he had landed without permission because he had been stupid enough to run out of fuel.

"Come in young man," the rancher said.

As Anton blurted out his story the old man walked over a sideboard.

"What's your name, son?"

"Anton."

"Right, Anton, drink this," he said handing him a tumbler of neat whisky. "If you managed to land out there without killing yourself, you probably need it."

Anton asked if he could use the phone as he needed to call home and let us know where he was.

"Sure, and get them to bring some overnight gear. You can't leave that plane out there. If the cattle get to it, they'll chew it to bits."

(This is where I take over the story).

When I got the telephone call I was relieved to know that Anton was safe. We hadn't started worrying because we just thought he'd stayed on at the flying club to have a beer or two with his flying buddies.

I listened carefully as I mulled over what would be needed. Camping gear; food – some stew we were going to have for supper could go into a flask; torches; sleeping bags.... Simon was hanging around insisting he was going out to camp out with his dad.

Our next door neighbour, Bill, was another home-build enthusiast, so I went round to ask him for help and about an hour later, Bill, Simon and I set off to find the ranch.

Embarrassed and inebriated with the whisky, Anton met us and, with the rancher, we made our way back to the plane.

By the time we reached the spot, a fog or sea mist had swept in from the ocean and confused the location. Eventually we found the airplane looking very forlorn surrounded by thick vegetation and made our way down the steep slope to it, carrying the overnight gear – our shadows looming enormous against the wall of fog lit by the torches we carried. After seeing Simon and Anton settled, Bill, the rancher and I drove away leaving them to the darkness and the distant howl of coyotes.

Bill and I returned to the crash landing area early next morning. Bill hadn't said he was very worried about the idea of Anton flying the plane out. He recognised the danger that Anton could crash and hurt himself – or even get killed. Instead he just told me he would come and help.

The day dawned clear and hot. The sky was a perfect blue with only thin wisps of cloud when we found Simon and Anton. They had already been hard at work clearing a 'runway'. Once they disturbed a snake, and while Anton shot back in fright, Simon kindly explained it was only a King Snake and therefore harmless.

Bill and Anton agreed that in spite of the light fuselage, they needed to make the plane even lighter.

Anton said he thought we should pull the plane as far up the hill as possible and then he would rev the engine as high as it would go while we held on to the tailplane.

"When I yell 'let go' jump back and I'll taxi off. I've picked an abort spot. If the plane is not flying then, I'll cut the engine and we'll have to take it to bits to get it out of here," Anton instructed.

Engine cowling, seat cushions and clothing were piled alongside camping gear. Anton climbed into the cockpit. Simon and I held on to the tailplane while Bill stood by to swing the propeller.

"Contact," shouted Anton. Bill swung the propeller and leapt back to join Simon and me, while Anton held the little plane on the brakes and wound the power up. He raised his arm and the three of us let go. The plane gathered speed, hurtling down the slope – but not fast enough as rocks and scrub slowed it down.

Bill began shouting, "Abort! Abort – now!" Anton later told us that in his anxiety to get airborne he'd forgotten his own mark and allowed the little plane to rush on towards a deep ravine. In desperation, he pulled back the stick, only thinking that he could do a pancake landing on the other side.

Miraculously, the aircraft cleared the terrifying drop into the abyss, sailed over the ravine and began to fly. Wheels bouncing over the scrub, this amazing piece of machinery flew up the slope gathering speed. It was only a few feet off the ground as it came to the top of the hill, too low to fly over the power cables ahead, so Anton flew under them and away, giving a 'wing waggle' as he passed over us on his way to the flying club and breakfast.

Later Bill said he'd watched, hardly daring to draw breath, while Simon stood there cheering. I almost fainted from the whole ordeal.

Bill, Simon and I then were faced with all the equipment which was still a hundred yards down in the canyon and had to be dragged up to our cars.

Although we were all very relieved Anton had made it, I was pretty annoyed when he accused us of 'taking our time' in joining up with him at San Juan Capistrano Flying Club.

Baseball and Soccer

I have always entered into helping out with the various sports my sons were involved with. When we moved to Mission Viejo I helped out with the Baseball Little League, eventually taking on the job of teaching other mothers how to keep score! *I* had to be taught first because I didn't have a clue. My next project was to become a football referee. The local children went from three hundred wanting to play one season to three thousand the next.

One of the American dads said to me, "You are English and so you must know something about soccer."

"I played hockey," I replied.

"That's close enough," he said and I was issued with a black and white, (men's) uniform. Fortunately we owned three pairs of football boots so that if Simon, Sean and I were all involved at the same time we didn't have to share. One pair, which fitted both Sean and me, were very comfortable and if we both needed them at the same time, Sean would wear them to bed the night before to stop me getting them!

The two Diana's

It was during this time that I became friends with two other mothers', strangely enough they were both named Diana. Both were equally *mad* in their own ways.

Diana Grey used to come regularly to have her cards read and I recall one afternoon particularly. I have always avoided telling of death or divorce – I could always be wrong, but on this occasion I told Diana to expect a death.

"It is not a relative," I said, "But I do think you will be upset. I am only telling you because I think Donald (her husband) is going to get promotion because of it." That was at 4.30pm. At six o'clock she phoned me.

"Anna, you will never believe this but last night Donald's boss committed suicide and Donald has been promoted because of it."

Great Western Savings

Diana Grey had three children and it was she who persuaded me to work in a Savings and Loan, a bit like a Building Society in England.

We met for lunch at a local Mexican restaurant, except that we never got round to eating. After two or three martinis, American style, she told me there was a job going at Great Western Savings where she worked and tried to persuade me to apply for the job. I thought it was funny because I had failed every maths exam I'd ever taken and I certainly didn't think I was cut out for banking. However she did encourage me to fill out an application form.

In those days if you were married you had to say what your husband did. (I suppose if I had written 'bank robber' they wouldn't have taken me on.) I wrote down that Anton sold boats, but after three martinis the 'b' looked a bit like a 'g'. The manager interviewed me straight away and the conversation went like this:

"That's very interesting, I've never met anyone who did this before," said the manager. That's odd, I thought, lots of people sell boats in southern California.

"Where does he sell them?"

"All over the world," I told him.

"What are they like?"

"Very luxurious."

"How much do they sell for?"

"They start at $25,000."

"$25,000 for a *goat!*" the astonished manager blurted out. We had been talking a cross purposes throughout the interview, but he offered me the job!

Halloween at Great Western Savings

We were allowed, in fact encouraged, to dress up in costume for Halloween, that is until they discovered bank robberies went up because you couldn't tell who was staff and who was a robber. One year I decided to go dressed as a witch. Type casting my family said. I found a very tatty old grey wig in the acting box and added that to the black dress and witch's hat. I then took a great deal of trouble doing my make-up, including highlighting the veins on the back of my hands – and I was running late for work. Driving over the speed limit on a back road while dashing to Great Western Savings, I was pulled over by a cop. He said nothing about my outfit, just,

"You were speeding, why?"

"My make-up took longer than usual," I replied.

"Let me see your driving license."

"I don't look much like the photo on it."

"No lady you don't!" he said as he handed me a $10 fine.

On the same day Anton took his Spanish Boat Dealer to meet the manager of the company's branch only to find him running around dressed as a chicken. It was very confusing for the Spaniard.

Diana and Joe Crevier

The first meeting with the other Diana was through Little League baseball. Their son Bobby was about Simon's age and they played in the same team. They also had a daughter Sherrie and a younger son Christopher. But it was the cars that attracted Simon and me.

At the beginning of our friendship, Diana was driving a Lincoln Continental and she and her husband Joe, shared a Maserati Bora. In California you could make up your own number plates and Diana's was 'My Bora'. Later they bought a Ferrari – which in fact was the one used in the film 'Gumball Rally'.

When I first met Diana I thought she was very glamorous. Red hair and always dressed to kill. Diana always walked in a sort of drifting manner, expecting to turn heads, which she did. Later, when she had dyed her hair black, she often wore it dressed like a Japanese geisha.

She, Joe and family lived not too far away from us. Joe dug swimming pools and we were most impressed by their two swimming pools. It was actually one pool with a waterfall down into the second. The Jacuzzi beside it caused a bit of a stir one evening!

It was a hot summer evening when Diana invited me over for a barbecue while Anton was away on a business trip. She had invited a group of their Ferrari friends as well. After sitting in semi-darkness, in their 'den', drinking glass after glass of wine and listening to Pink Floyd in quadraphonic sound, we were ready to hit the Jacuzzi. I got out my bikini to put on and Diana said,

"Have you washed that in a regular washing machine Anna?" I answered yes I had.

"Well I'm afraid you can't wear that in the pool because it will still have remnants of soap powder which could affect the mechanics." I listened to her – *and stupidly*, or was it the effect of the wine, believed her. It was only later when we'd all been skinny dipping that she let on she conned me! There was absolutely no reason at all why I couldn't wear my bathing things in her Jacuzzi. She still laughs about it to this day.

Those heady days stretched into months and years, gradually tapering off as the times changed and we became older. By the time I was thirty-one, several of the close community had moved away from the neighbourhood. We had all made other friends and the early frantic 'got to get to know everyone' was over.

Do I regret those wild times in southern California? Sometimes. There are still some things I am embarrassed about. There are things I look back on and wish I hadn't done, but I can't go back and change things.

Our Neighbour and his Soccer Team

I still look back on this evening with some remorse as to what we did to the house opposite ours. Mr Adams, the owner, was the coach of one of the rival under-sixteen football teams. Simon's team and the Adam's met in the final. Mr Adams pulled a few fast ones and his team won. Our team, the boys, the parents and other children retired to the local pizza place to drown our sorrows. We got there at about 4.00pm. By nine o'clock we had all downed rather a lot of beer. Several of the kids wanted to go to a movie and someone took them, with the understanding I would pick them up later. In the meantime, some of the other mothers, and I of course, decided to go and 'T-P' the Adams house. 'T-Peeing' stands for toilet papering. We all went to our own homes and collected rolls of toilet paper and in the dark rendezvoused outside the front of the Adams house ready to decorate the trees and bushes. I had never thrown a loo roll before – it is actually very difficult because the weight of the roll causes the paper to tear at the perforated bits. With lots of stifled giggles and dashing behind bushes whenever a car drove past, we managed to make a fair old mess of his front garden.

One of the mums felt a bit bad about what we'd done and went home and got a pot plant to leave on his doorstep as a sort of peace offering. The problem with toilet paper is when it gets wet it is impossible to get off the bushes again and this lot did get wet. The automatic sprinkler system designed to come on at dawn the following morning thoroughly soaked everything!

Later, that night, as I was getting ready for bed I received a plaintive call from Simon asking where I was. I had forgotten all about them. On the way back from collecting them, we passed the Adams house and the kids exclaimed when they saw the mess.

"Oh, look, someone has T-Peed Mr Adam's house!"

"That was me and your mum, Tom, and your mum, Phil etc." They didn't believe me, when I insisted. They just thought it was the alcohol talking.

Next morning I woke up with a massive hangover and a terrible memory of what we had done. I phoned Tom's mum.

"I know," she said, "but I have been thinking about it and have come to the conclusion that nobody would ever believe it was us, secondly I will never do it again and thirdly, I found out why the kids do it because it was actually great fun!"

An hour later, when I stopped at our local petrol station to fill my car up, who should drive in, with a face as black as thunder, but Mr Adams? I panicked because I thought he had already found out and was coming to get me. He hadn't of course, but I could tell he was absolutely furious. *I* also, have never done it again.

The E-Type Jaguar

We bought a white E-type Jaguar and enjoyed it very much before selling it. Unfortunately for us, one month after the sale, Jaguar announced they were no longer going to build this car and the value shot up. We were told by an English former Jag mechanic that it was one of the very early models as it had beaten aluminium on the dashboard instead of the fancy polished wood. It also had the original headlamps. I loved it and once drove up the wrong freeway because a guy in a red Mustang came alongside and we diced (not very fast!) each other. It was only after about twenty miles that I realised what I'd done and then had to cut across Garden Grove from the Santa Ana to the San Diego freeway. It took ages.

One evening when we had been out we came back to find the Jag missing from our drive. I had left the keys in the ignition. Worried, because we were so close to the Mexican border, we were afraid someone had pinched it to sell over there. Next morning I phoned my friend Dottie Peterson to ask for help. She prepared an astrology chart for the time I had asked the question. Next morning she called back and told me the chart revealed that the car had been stolen by the *child of a neighbour and was at that moment parked on a hill, outside a big building, which might be a school or a hospital and it was approximately 5.8 miles to the west*. We thanked her, not really believing the prediction. I then asked if Anton hired an airplane and flew over the area on the following Saturday would he find it? – it was such a distinctive car. Next day she phoned again – No, he shouldn't bother because we would know what had happened to it before then.

Next morning – Thursday, I received an extraordinary phone call from the police. They had got our car. The fifteen year old son of a neighbour had been stopped when he was speeding. At the time of my first question the car had been parked outside his school, which was on a hill, approximately 5.8 miles to the west! Even Dottie said she had never been so accurate before.

My next car was a Honda Civic. I came over to England that summer for a couple of weeks and while I was away, discovered later, that Sean had not only been driving my car, he was thirteen at the time, but he'd even had the cheek to give driving lessons to his friends – and charging them for it!

The Hobie-Cat

The man who designed the Hobie-cat was one of Anton's flying buddies. His original catarman was a fourteen foot model but we bought a sixteen foot one with a jib. It was a fantastic catamaran until you tried to tack in strong winds, when it could capsize forwards, tripping over itself, but sailed in normal waters it moved extremely fast.

Hawaii here I come

If I had known then what I know now, I would never have agreed to go sailing that afternoon. A friend from Northern California was visiting his elderly mother and I accepted his request for a sail on our Hobie 16. Bill had never been sailing before so it was not the best time to learn as the conditions were hardly ideal.

We launched the cat at Dana Point Harbour. It was windy but didn't seem that bad – that is, until we sailed out from behind the breakwater. Then it hit us. Hobie cats can be hairy in any weather but as we got further out the wind seemed to increase and the boat really began to pound through and over the waves. The spray from the boat mixed with the white spume being blown off the top of the dark water of the Pacific Ocean almost blinding us, as the sixteen foot boat hurtled from one crest to another and another.

Then my troubles really began. I couldn't get the boat to tack for us to return to the safety of the harbour. I attempted the manoeuvre three or four times, having to pull back at the last minute and with each attempt my fear grew. At one point I thought, Hawaii here I come! The waves were getting bigger and steeper and the troughs deeper. There were no other boats so far out. I thought we were going to die. In desperation when the next large trough appeared I yelled at Bill to haul in on the jib sheet and then to throw himself across the boat. Miraculously the cat spun round and very quickly picked up terrific speed and we were racing back with me hanging on with every ounce of my strength. The boat rode the top of the waves like a surfer. I didn't dare ask Bill to put on the trapeze and stand on the windward side of the hull, preferring to ease the mainsail to spill wind in order to slow us down, but not for long. One quick glance back showed a sky getting darker by the minute as the storm chased us home. Waves were now breaking down their front and I expected any minute that one of them would break over us. Desperate to get to safety I let the boat go, wind and waves fighting each other, while I fought to keep us stable.

Then suddenly the wind died as we rounded into the shelter of the harbour and the cat settled quietly down on the smoother water. I eased the mainsail rope from the crushing grip round my hand, now marked with rope burns from allowing it to slip as I tried to hang on.

We were not the only fools who had braved the weather that day. Three other boats limped in with broken rudders and one with a broken mast. We were lucky.

"That was great! Can we go out again?"

"You don't know how close to death you came" was my shaky reply as tears of relief mingled with cold salt water dripping from my soaking wet hair.

Sailing with Whales

One time, when we were sailing near Dottie Peterson's amazing house which was perched on a rock overhanging the Pacific Ocean, the whales were migrating from Alaskan waters to the calm bay off Baja California in Mexico where they give birth to their calves. These gigantic, magnificent creatures were just gently cruising down the coast in shoals. One enormous whale was so close to us on the Hobie-cat that we decided to try and get even closer. We sailed as carefully and quietly as we could, moving closer to the huge creature, until we were only a couple of feet away from its vast body. Very tentatively I reached out and ran my hand over the barnacled grey skin. The whale made no immediate reaction until suddenly it blew from its spout and the most terrible smell of rotting fish hit our nostrils!

Another Move

By now American Marine was in trouble and we sold our house and moved, for a year only, to a small condominium in El Toro, slightly further north. For the second move running, Anton managed to be away on a business trip! Fortunately this time his airplane was not tucked away in the garage but tied down at San Juan Capistrano airfield.

CHAPTER 14

MISSION VIEJO AGAIN

The Townhouse

This was my favourite home in southern California – it was very classy. Perhaps I thought of it this way because it has been the only house I have ever lived where I was in at the beginning, choosing it originally from the plans, picking out the carpets and curtains. I felt it was mine.

One of my very best memories of that time was an evening soon after we moved in. I sat alone on the mid-level balcony of the townhouse, enjoying the taste and aroma of an ice-cold glass of Zinfandel, a delicious Californian white wine, and listening to the cicadas chirping in an almost sing song purr.

I felt the warmth of the evening and was aware of a slight breeze rustling the leaves or petals of the soft peach bougainvillea below. It was my favourite colour. Scent of gardenias filtered through the night sky and I felt contented. – not something I experienced often in those days.

Behind me the townhouse was new and the smell fresh and unspoilt. I knew that, under the star filled quiet darkness, the greens and fairways of a private golf course bridged the gap between us and the freeway, which at night was wonderful to watch as the lights of home going traffic flowed unceasingly in the distance.

About the only negative thing was that, being built on three stories, it was tiring to take care of.

We had two phones, one listed to Anton and I and one to The Emmerton Boys. One day when I was at work I attempted to phone home – their phone was busy. I tried on my phone and it was busy.

159

When I eventually got through, Simon told me that Sean, who was on the lowest floor, had been too lazy to walk up to the bedroom floor to speak to his brother so he had phoned him on the other line!

They also got me in trouble when they ventured on to the course and waited until a golfer left his buggy to walk over to his ball and then they would sneak up, jump into the buggy and drive it away!

Fairways Marine

American Marine no longer existed as far as we were concerned. The two Newton brothers, the founders, had been pushed aside, along with Anton and Tony Nedderman. Tony Fleming was still in charge of the boat building side and the former American accountant, Bob Livingstone, took over the day to day running of the company, which was still based in Singapore.

Anton needed to work and so he approached Fairways Marine, a Hamble based British boat builder. Although the style was completely different because the Fishers were sailing vessels, in many ways they were similar in that the Fairways Fisher and the Grand Banks were both heavy displacement, comfortable cruising boats. Anton was employed to sell the Fishers all over the United States and so we stayed on there.

Richard Lyon Clark, a lovely American who reminded me so much of James Stewart, the Hollywood actor, became the advertising man for the Fishers. He was very clever and the words he used on his ads were always very enticing to, at least, go for a trial sail. We sold one of our biggest boats to Buzz Aldrin, among the first astronauts to land on the moon.

Coffins and Caskets

When Anton was talking to Tony Fleming one day, bemoaning the public and the warranty problems on their boats, Anton said to Tony,

"What can we build out of wood where there won't be any warranty problems?"

As a joke the idea of building caskets and coffins came to them and within six months the first prototypes were shipped over from Singapore.

I clearly recall the evening when we showed our beautiful caskets to two salesmen in an effort to persuade them to promote them round the big funeral parlours. Our models were exact half replicas. We had three different types of wood – mahogany, iroko and oak. I found some velvet fabric to drape over a table and Anton arranged the lighting to show the caskets in their best light.

The two salesmen arrived. The one who took on our line was called *Mort*. He really was! But he had no sense of humour. When he and his friend looked at our display, Mort turned and said,

"Aren't they beautiful? Can you image if they were lined with some decorated silk. Something to give the impression of the sky, or of woods, or the ocean - we could even have some hand embroidered lettering inside. Now what was it Martin Luther King said? 'Freedom at last!' " At this moment I collapsed with the giggles because all I could think of was the lid coming down on me and being far from free! I had to run out of the room because they were being serious.

Actually we did hear of other firms having warranty problems. One that made me laugh was when the coffin bearers were carrying another manufacturer's casket. Inside was a very heavy, dead of course, young man and as the bearers struggled to the graveside, he fell out of the bottom and landed at this mother's feet. What made it worse was that he was in one of the special burial suits made for open casket ceremony's and although it looked perfect from the front, it was not enclosed at the back and so he literally did fall on *his* bottom. His mother sued that firm for millions!

Another bizarre but true Californian story was told by a friend. She had been invited to visit a deceased lady at the funeral parlour on Thursday afternoon. When she arrived she was staggered to find the lady beautifully dressed and made-up and sitting in a chair – dead as a dodo!

It soon became apparent Anton needed help in the office and so I gave up yet another job, Adventures in Achievement, and joined him. Actually we got on very well in the office, the only real thing that infuriated me was that he would give me my pay cheque, insist that I endorse it over to him and then put it in his bank account, doling out my housekeeping from it.

Belts and Chains

Because the boats were made in England and shipped over, we began work at 7.00am and finished at 3.30pm because of the eight hour time difference.

One afternoon at about 3.25pm, when I was preparing to pack up for the day, a woman came to the door, not to see me, but to meet up with the man who was a printer and who occupied the centre section of our warehouse. We sold boats from the front, coffins and caskets from the back and Jim was in the middle.

On this particular afternoon Jim was out. I didn't know if he was returning because his was a completely separate business and I couldn't go off without locking up. I took pity on this lady because she was very hot and sticky. The temperature on that mid July day was really high and she had nowhere to go to wait. She had not come by car, but had managed to get a bus – something quite difficult in southern California! I offered her a cup of coffee and agreed to wait for a little while.

Then the weirdest thing happened. It was as if someone was telling me to tell her that they were very glad she had reformed her way of life. This astonished me because she was hardly attractive, and was probably somewhere in her mid fifties and very plump. However, I did tell her and, not batting an eyelid she asked me who it was. Over the following half an hour at least twenty five different things came through. She had been called after the old lady who'd appeared in my mind. The house was three stories high with a raised wooden porch and a dirt track outside. The woman in front of me kept saying that it sounded like her grandmother's house but none of the facts matched. Soon after, she left.

A few days later I was surprised to receive a phone call from her.

"You were a hundred percent accurate. Everything you said was

162

true, and it *was* my grandmother. I didn't recognise some of the things because she died when I was only three. It had been a dirt road which was surfaced before I was born, and it was three stories and so on."

Then she reminded me that I had said her grandmother seemed happy and I agreed, but reminded her that the old lady had come out clearly with the message that she was pleased her granddaughter had reformed her way of life. It was at this point I was glad we were communicating over the phone because I couldn't have kept a straight face. First of all she told me they were Catholics and they were not sure if her grandmother had been murdered or committed suicide. If it had been suicide the family were convinced she would have ended up in purgatory. I opted for suicide because I felt the old lady had been watching over her granddaughter for the past five years and it certainly seemed like purgatory to her.

"Oh," she said, "you are absolutely right. Five years ago I abandoned my family, including my children and got involved in all sorts of things - drugs, alcohol and sex. Not just straight sex, but group sex and lesbianism, but the only thing I didn't do was belts and chains!" I had this sudden image of the poor old lady watching over her granddaughter and trying to keep track of things. I had to hold my nose to stop myself laughing.

Adventures in Achievement

While working at Great Western Savings, I was taken to hear Jim Rohn speak at a three hour session. What he said changed my life. He talked about the positive and negative things in life and why some people succeed and some fail. I walked out of that meeting wondering how Jim Rohn knew so much about me – but then so did most of the other five hundred people. I was so impressed that I gave up my job at Great Western Savings and went to join the salesmen and women of Adventures in Achievement and although I eventually came to the conclusion I would never be a direct salesman, I have never regretted going because it shaped my future and helped me to forge a career in Sales Training. Two of Jim Rohn's sayings are with me today:

"Let death find me climbing a new mountain" and

"There is the right job for everyone, the problem is finding it, but if you keep an open mind and are willing to listen and learn, then sometimes it comes in a blinding flash. It may be something you hear, or read or see, that triggers it off and you say to yourself – that's I, that's what I'm going to do."

Now I am not sure what triggered it off in my mind but one morning at about 4.30am I woke up and knew that I wanted to teach others how to sell. I realised I hated selling but wanted to take all the ideas I'd collected over the year and a half I had worked for Jim Rohn and use them to help other people. I climbed straight out of bed, began going through all my notes and a year and a half later I taught my first class in my dining room back in England – but that's another story.

While working for Adventures in Achievement I attended a weekend seminar in northern California. On one afternoon we sat down and wrote out our goals for every part of our life, especially career goals. I remember writing down that I wanted to have our house in California and a country cottage in England. What I forgot to say that I wanted to go on living in California. A year after writing this down, we, as a family, moved back to the UK and kept the Californian property for another year.

This time we moved the Volkesplane and the three-quarter scale Spitfire Anton had begun working on back to a cold November England.

CHAPTER 15
RETURN TO ENGLAND, 1981

Marleycombe

Fairways Marine was floundering and they decided to bring us back to England so that Anton could work out of the head office at Hamble, just outside Southampton.

Anton found us a pretty thatched cottage in the village of Bowerchalke in the Chalke Valley, south of Salisbury, Wiltshire. The house was built on the side of a slope and had been extended at both ends which made each room lower than the one next to it. It dropped about six steps/feet in total. The bank was so steep that, at our bedroom end, the front window was on the first floor but the side window was only four feet from the ground.

A couple of years later I was scared to death when I woke up one night to see, what I thought was a man, climbing through the window. I imagined it was his shoulders silhouetted against the night sky. Trembling I stared at the shape when it suddenly gave a great bellow! A cow was looking in at me and I found the garden filled with our neighbouring farmer's cattle.

We moved into the house in November. I remember how *cold* it was after eleven years of warmth in southern California. I think I hugged the Aga cooker in the kitchen for most of the first few months. I know Simon, especially, loved Marleycombe, but I always felt it was a sad house and it never seemed to let anyone stay for very long. The people who bought it from us planned to retire and live there for life, but they moved on only a year or two after they moved in.

Simon and Sean were enrolled at Kelly College in Tavistock. I really didn't want them to go away to boarding school but Anton insisted. It was actually Simon's skill in counting in binary that won them the places because the headmaster was very impressed by him. They were there for three years and I think Sean enjoyed it more than Simon, although they both made some good friends. One of whom frightened me considerably when I caught him sniffing Anton's very powerful airplane glue out of a five gallon container.

Anton's airplanes

A year or so after we moved I began teaching Estate Agents. One of the things I taught the participants was that there were many reasons for buying a property – hobbies being one of them. This was certainly Anton's view. It didn't actually matter how many bedrooms or reception rooms we had, the important thing was that there was sufficient room for his airplanes. The advantage of Marleycombe was a large wooden barn at one side of the drive. Unfortunately Anton discovered, after we moved in, there was no electricity hooked up to the barn and decided to change his plans.

I remember the conversation clearly when he checked out the ground floor of the house itself. He said that if he took the windows out, and I mean *really* out, frames and all, he could get the plane into the 'L' shaped room. The other part of this room was a downstairs bathroom. When people asked if they could use the lavatory, I used to tell them to watch out for the airplane. Generally, if they didn't know about Anton's hobby, they would come back and say, "You really do have an airplane in there!"

Later when Anton was ready to begin building the wings, but hadn't completed the fuselage, he phoned from work one day to say he'd figured it out that *if we moved into the spare bedroom and tipped our bed up against the wall, he could build the wings in the bedroom!* Fortunately it didn't come to that as there was no way he could get them out when finished, without pulling down a wall.

Dinner Parties at Marleycombe

My sister Jo well remembered the dinner parties we gave. Many a time I phoned her to check her deep freeze, or phoned the butcher to persuade him to go back into his shop after hours, to get me some meat because Anton had decided to bring someone, or on occasion, several people home for dinner. He would say they would stop and have a drink en route and would arrive home in about an hour and a half! It wouldn't have been so bad if he'd ever given me my housekeeping on time.

The butcher's shop was almost opposite the large house formerly owned by Cecil Beaton. His father recalled the times when Greta Garbo had been staying the Cecil and had walked across the road to borrow the butcher's dog to take it for a walk.

Spray Polish

Anton liked to tell me what housework I had to do during the day and I'd often get orders about what I should accomplish while he was at work. I recall one morning when he gave me my instructions. I knew from past experiences there was no point in arguing with him. I needed to go out but I also knew that Anton was planning to go sailing after work and wouldn't be back until at least 9.00pm. It's OK, I thought, I'll get back early and do the chores before he arrives home. Unfortunately I was out longer than I'd planned to be. At about 6.15pm, when I was beginning to dust and polish, I looked out of the front window and to my cold horror, I saw him driving up. As quick as a flash I turned the can and proceeded to cover *myself* with the spray polish. I met Anton at the front door where he sniffed appreciatively,

"Umm, the house does smell nice, you must have worked hard today." I followed him from room to room. He believed I had dusted the whole house, he never noticed that the polish was all over me!

The Green Amazon Parrot

Anton's sister, Janice, acquired a parrot from an old lady who could no longer take care of it. The female bird was called Jo and used to shriek this name whenever she became excited. I hasten to add that the parrot was not called after my sister, but was already called Jo when Janice acquired her. Unfortunately Janice did not like the parrot and I think made it even more paranoid, so Anton brought it home one day. It was not particularly friendly to anyone except Sean whom it never bit. He would let it walk up and down his arm and feed it individual raw peas which it would carefully peel the skins off, eat the middle and throw the skin on the floor.

I was terrified of Jo who attacked me on several occasions, once when I was washing up. Jo managed to get herself out of her cage which hung in the kitchen, and flew straight at my feet. She grabbed the bottom of my trousers and began pecking and biting. Not wanting to put my hand down to fend her off, I filled a saucepan with cold water and tipped it over her - thoroughly soaking myself at the same time. Jo let go to shake herself off and I managed to persuade her to climb on a broom handle before restoring her to her cage.

In the evenings Anton insisted on bringing the parrot into the sitting room with us, she enjoyed the company, he said. This lasted until one memorable night when Anton was assembling a model balsa wood airplane. As soon as he left the room for a few minutes, Jo clambered down from the back of the chair she was perched on, climbed up the table leg, and by the time Anton reappeared was sitting among the remains of the model, tearing it to bits and shrieking, "Hallo Jo!" That did it - next day I phoned a pet shop in Salisbury who specialised in birds, especially parrots, and Jo went to a new home. She was only a young bird and they hoped to breed from her.

I was told later that, although she was uncomfortable with other parrots to begin with, as she had always lived on her own among humans, she had integrated really well and was living with numerous other parrots, still shouting 'Hallo Jo!'

Den's Mini

Anton's stepfather was dying of cancer. He was only sixty-one when he died. As Dolly, Anton's mother no longer had any use for her Mini, because she took over Den's car, they gave it to me. It had a number of things wrong with it; the petrol gauge didn't work and I kept a piece of cane in the car, which I dipped into the tank to see how far up the stick the petrol came! Its other problem was that it leaked like a sieve, which I found out when I took it through a car wash. The water poured in through every conceivable gap and there was nothing I could do but sit there, laugh and get soaked. I had to go home to change my wet clothes before going into the supermarket with the back of my skirt looking as though I'd had a nasty accident!

Sadly Den died, I kept the Mini and continued to drive it. One day when I was heading for Southampton I was pulled over by a policeman. The offence was not having a current license visible on the windscreen. I told him a lie and said the offending Tax disk was in my desk at home. The policeman walked round my car and pointed to one of my rear tyres and told me it was below the legal limit.

I responded with, "That makes me really annoyed because I've just had a new tyre fitted on the front, why didn't the garage tell me at the time I needed another new one!"

"Didn't it occur to you to check your tyres yourself madam?"

I politely said, "Don't you think that's a pretty silly question to ask any woman? How many women do you know who even check how much petrol they've got, let alone the tyres?"

He agreed it was a silly question and let me go with instructions to present myself at the police station in Salisbury with the two things put right. Unfortunately I didn't have a Tax disk because my mother-in-law had mislaid the M.O.T. certificate and without it I couldn't renew the license.

It was the time of the petrol shortage in England in 1980 or thereabouts and because I didn't present myself at the police station the local bobby cycled out from Salisbury to interview me not having enough petrol to drive out to Bowerchalke.

169

First I had to admit that I hadn't taxed the car because we could not find the M.O.T. certificate. Upon hearing that the owner of the car was now deceased he told me I should have been given written permission to drive the car before the owner, Anton's step-father died. Then he discovered that I was still driving on a Californian driving license – I should have replaced it with an English one within one year of returning to the UK. In all I broke eight laws! But in the end I received a nice letter from the local constabulary, outlining the offences and telling me I was let off this time and not to do it again. It must have been all the tea and cakes I entertained the cycling bobby with when he visited me on three separate occasions! My butcher was furious I'd got away with breaking so many laws and he'd been fined £10 for only the one offence, one worn tyre.

Janice and her Car

Janice, Anton's sister, is a lovely woman but not very mechanically minded. I remember a classic case when Janice arrived at her mother's house one afternoon. She was anxious and out of breath when she exclaimed, "Oh, Mummy, I had to drive so fast to get here!"

"Why did you need to drive so fast Janice?" my mother-in-law asked. Janice was only bringing her children to have tea with us.

"I had to drive fast because I was running out of petrol, and I wanted to get here before I ran out!"

It took us a while to explain how an engine works – and to stop laughing.

Another day she arrived having run into the back of the car in front of her.

"Well I didn't know he was going to stop!"

"Weren't you looking Janice?" asked her brother Anton.

"No, I was leaning down and picking something up from the floor of my car and so I didn't notice the lights had changed."

The Citroen Diane

After the Mini died, Anton bought me a Citroen Diane – a more infuriating car I have never come across. It was not only uncomfortable, especially in the back seat, but it was so under powered I became extremely *frustrated*! The only way I could overtake lorries was going down hill flat out, and then find them overtaking me again on uphill slopes.

My children, especially Sean, loved to drive this awful French car – although I wasn't aware he was using it. It was after visiting Hugh and Janet Pickford, farming friends who lived in Broadchalke, that I became conscious of the smell of manure every time the car warmed up a bit. Later I tracked it down to the afternoon, when, while I was having tea with Janet, Sean had been driving my car round the slurry yard. The underside was totally caked with cow muck and whenever the engine heated up so the smell increased!

Simon has since reminded me that one evening several of them had taken my car, drove it to the pub, where the lads got quite drunk, and then on the way home, they visited the local trout hatchery and pinched a number of fairly large trout. I only found out about it when I went into my bathroom the following morning and found them swimming around in the bath! I got them out of bed so fast, shouting that they should take the damn trout back immediately!

Momentum Training

Before I left California I decided to become a Sales Trainer. I never enjoyed the actual selling of goods with the cold calling and telephone sales.

By the time we had been back in England for about a year I was ready with my training course, which I held in the dining room at Marleycombe. Six people attended and I was off and running.

During that time I sat in the garden and wrote down my list of goals, one of which was that I would be teaching nationwide within twelve months. Pretty ambitious! But, having written it down, surprising things began to happen. I was already heading towards training Estate Agents and after talking to someone connected with one of the Estate Agency magazines, I found myself being taken on by the Polytechnic of Central London on Marylebone Road and for the next two years I travelled up to London to teach a series of classes. The biggest group numbered 350 students.

It was during this class that I almost lost control of the group. We were doing a Motivation exercise where the delegates were asked to grade themselves in various aspects, one of which was 'Physical'. I said that this meant 'physical fitness'.

One young man put his hand up and asked, 'Does this include my sex life?' I replied, 'Well it depends how fit you feel.' He looked me straight in the eye and said, 'Before – or afterwards?' Needless to remark, it brought the house down.

From there I worked for the Incorporated Society of Valuers and Auctioneers, The National Association of Estate Agents and many individual firms all over the country, from Scotland, England, Wales and also Ireland and Jersey and was a guest speaker at various conferences.

Anton Returned to the USA

Fairways Marine was failing and Anton decided he would go back to California to start a new career. He joined up with Dick Clark to produce a versatile dinghy, which they called the Carib-Dory.

Anton left, I thought, on Good Friday and the kids and I threw a weekend long party to celebrate his leaving. Looking back on it I feel very sorry for our neighbours in Bowerchalke because we were all very loud and wild that weekend. However when I was taking one of the boys to the train station on Monday afternoon, I saw Anton driving towards me. I was horrified as I thought he was well ensconced in the States. He had actually gone off to spend the weekend in North Devon with a girlfriend I didn't even know about and hadn't planned to leave until the following Wednesday.

Anyway, on the Wednesday he did depart, leaving me with no

money and two boys in boarding school and a mortgage to cope with. Inevitably I was forced to sell the house and the boys left Kelly College.

Sean wanted to return to California to complete his High School education so he could attend university over there. Although Anton now lived in Newport Beach, Sean did not go to live with him but moved in with Sally Williams and family, who were by then living in South Laguna. Simon came with me.

I found a rented house in Warsash, just outside Southampton, where we remained for a while until Simon also returned to California to stay with his father. I have to say I was relieved because some of Simon's friends at that time were pretty bad.

It was at this time I was invited to speak at an Incorporated Society of Valuers and Auctioneers conference at Stratford-upon-Avon and it was here I met my second husband, Michael Rains, although I do not remember that meeting. He told me, when we met at the same conference the following year in Pitlochry, that he hadn't forgotten me. I was thirty-nine at the time.

Before going to Cheshire in 1983, I moved to Chandlers Ford, just north of Southampton, to stay with my sister, her husband, daughter and my mother for a few months.

CHAPTER 16
CHESHIRE 1983

Brook House Farm

I moved to Brook House Farm in mid November 1983. It is a lovely old Cheshire farmhouse, built in 1760 and located in the golden triangle between Wilmslow, Alderley Edge and Prestbury, (known by this name because of the number of extremely wealthy people living in the area).

We live in Mottram St Andrew, which is still predominantly a farming community, although, in 2005, it was being taken over by the nouveau riche, many of whom are Premiership footballers. Since I first wrote this book, many houses have been bought for £1 million or more and then flattened to build even bigger and more amazing properties.

Michael

My mother always said that it didn't matter what a person looked like or what they did in life, but the one thing you couldn't live without is *kindness* and Michael is very, very kind and very attractive. I was thirty-nine and he was fifty-nine when we met.

Wherever we go on holiday he sends postcards - dozens of them. I recall one occasion when he sent a card to a former office cleaning lady of his. She only had one son and Michael said he liked to send her postcards because he didn't think she received much mail and he imagined the arrival of the card would cheer her up. He was the head of a large firm of Estate Agents, and here he was trying to bring a bit of happiness into his cleaner's life!

Michael and I married on February 21st, 1987. It was a very happy – and sad day. Michael's brother Peter became a grandfather again, for the fourth time, his first grandson, who was born at 8.00am. We got married at noon and then one of Michael's first cousins, who came to the wedding, sat down at home and quietly slipped away. We had a birth, a wedding and a death in just eleven hours.

Simon and His Family

Simon returned from the States soon after I moved to Cheshire. He wasn't easy to cope with at this time but I am delighted to say that at the time of writing this book he is one of the nicest men you could find. He has *grown up!*

During his first year or so back from America he drifted with a crowd of young men, some of whom were involved with the drug scene. Then he moved to Wiltshire and found a job in a carpet manufacturing company, before going on to Southampton University to study computers. He excelled at this and was head-hunted by a firm which was looking for bright young men, and has continued in this line of work ever since. While he was there, he and another young man, were warned that the Principal was aware they had the ability to break into the main body of the university computer – but they'd better not!

In the meantime Simon met Anna. She was fifteen at the time and he was twenty-six. Two and a half years later, just after Anna's eighteenth birthday they got married on 10th February 1990 at Hindon in Wiltshire.

Anna was still in school and hadn't taken her 'A' Levels. When I queried the reason for the wedding she told me she decided to get married first, otherwise she would be thinking more about the wedding than her exams!.

I have fond memories of their wedding. First of all Simon phoned me to say he had volunteered me for two jobs. One – to read one of the lessons, Anna's mother Jenni read the other. My other job was to do the catering. "Prepare the food or pay for it?" was my question. "Both," replied Simon.

The reception took place in the village hall. Anna was asked to check out, in advance, the number of cookers in the kitchen. Three she said – but there was only one which worked. One was broken and the other was the fridge! Nevertheless I managed to prepare hot food for over one hundred people.

Before the wedding took place we were all dressed and ready when Simon asked my sister Jo to take a glass of brandy and a note to Anna's house just down the road. Jo did so, although she spilt the first glass in her car – she said. Jenni was horrified when Jo arrived with the note from Simon for Anna. She clearly thought he was going to do a runner! However the note merely said, 'I've forgotten my toothbrush!'

At the reception the top table was placed on the stage because the hall was rather small. Janice did all the flowers and the reception got under way with everyone enjoying themselves. Then we arrived at the time for the speeches, at which moment Anton, who had been stockpiling bread rolls, decided to throw one at Jenny Farrant. The young ones were astonished as adults took part in a bread roll fight! That was the end of any speeches.

Before going away on honeymoon, Anna changed into her 'going away' outfit. I must say she really had the men staring. She had chosen to wear a very short, skirt I think but it may have been hot pants, thigh length boots, a see through blouse and a big hat. I can still hear my former mother-in-law's intake of breath and her saying, "Why couldn't she have worn a nice little suit?"

Anna is a very intelligent and pretty girl, but somewhat eccentric, which became obvious at her wedding. After leaving school she enrolled at Art School to do fashion design. She and Simon were living, first on Jenny Farrant's farm and then in Hastings before relocating to Bristol where she completed her design course.

Anna was also head-hunted from college, this time by a local designer. About three months after she began working I asked her if she was doing any designing yet. She replied that she was learning to 'glue rubber'! Astonished, I enquired why and it turned out she was working for someone who made *fetish* clothes for a shop in Bristol. I always remember her telling me that Simon had refused to go to their fashion show. Simon replied, "I'm not surprised mum. The finale was a bloke in a see-through rubber kilt – only!" Later, Melzie loved going with Anna to the shop because the walls of the changing rooms were lined with pink fur.

On September 20th 1995, Melzie arrived. Michael and I were staying in our house in France when Simon telephoned to tell us of her birth.

"She is called Demelza Moth Emmerton," he said.

"Moth?"

"It's from Shakespeare, Mum."

Actually Melzie does look a little like a moth with large expressive eyes. Anyway it is much prettier than Peaseblossom, Cobweb or Mustardseed which are the names of the other fairies from a Midsummer Night's Dream!

At the time of the first writing Melzie had just celebrated her tenth birthday. She is an exceptional reader and I remember the day when I was staying with them and a lady came from Bristol University to interview Simon about her reading ability. Melzie was reading articles from the Guardian newspaper when she was only six years old! The lady asked Simon how she had acquired the skill, he replied that he and Anna had given her lots of books to read and she'd really taught herself.

Simon and Anna are no longer together and Melzie lives with Simon and at that time saw her mother several times a week. Sadly this is no longer true as Anna's eccentricity has led her into far from pleasant surroundings.

Melzie is now at Redlands High School in Bristol. It is a private girls school and she is excelling again – surprisingly in every subject, getting top marks in all areas from science to languages, art, drama, sports and especially maths.

Sean and his family

Sean, having returned to the United States, has lived there ever since. He met Lisa Lindquist and they were married in 1989. It was an amazing wedding which, unfortunately, was beyond Sean's income at the time and he spent years catching up with his debts.

Hunter McKenzie Sean was born on July 4th 1991. By this time they were living in Phoenix, Arizona, where Sean was working in the hotel business.

Lisa has an absolutely identical twin sister whose husband was a hotelier and because the girls liked to do everything the same, Sean joined the hotel business as well.

When Hunter was eight months old, Sean brought his family to England – to escape from his financial problems. They also brought Aggie, a little Lhasa Apso. Sean, Lisa and Hunter stayed with us for three months, and during this time they only ate one meal with us – on the first night, with Lisa preparing their food separately after that. I still think it was pretty strange.

Finally Sean managed to find a job at Hanbury Manor Hotel and they moved to Hitchin in Hertfordshire.

Lisa became pregnant again and Grace Marilyn Rose was born on 13th May 1993. Within a few weeks they were off again, returning to the United States.

It was during their time in Hitchin that finally turned Lisa off Simeon, Michael's younger son. Lisa had returned to California for a holiday when Sim and Dominic, an old school friend of Simon and Sean's went to stay with Sean for the weekend. At the end of the visit, Sean left for work, leaving Sim and Dominic to depart later. Returning home from work Sean was horrified to find his *friends* had *decorated* his house with pictures taken from a 'Playboy' magazine. These they placed in all of his windows – facing out. By the time he got home, Sim and Dom had left and the neighbours were up in arms. Lisa was naturally furious when she returned from holiday and was informed of the prank.

Sean and Lisa departed England as we were leaving for a three week trip to Canada and Alaska. They left Aggie behind and when we returned I collected her from the kennels and passed her on to Michael's sister Margaret.

It was also during this same holiday that we heard about Anton's death. We were cruising off the Alaskan coast when Simon contacted the ship. Anton had died of leukaemia, which nobody knew he had.

Several years later, after his mother's death, I went to her funeral.

Now bearing in mind there had been a cremation service in California, followed by a memorial service in East Knoyle, I was naturally astonished to find that the service sheet mentioned a funeral service for Dolly, his mother, and *another* service for Anton. I questioned Simon and he whispered he'd only just found out that his father's ashes were in the coffin with his mother! I don't know what Anton would have thought but Simon believed he would have preferred to have his ashes scattered over the desert in California.

Sean and his family spent some time in Hawaii, where he drove a limo, before returning to California. Anton St John Connor was born on 21st February 1995. Lisa had now caught up with her sister again – two boys and a girl.

Over the years they have prospered with Sean running his own business, now working in the vacation industry with responsibility for hotels and leisure centres in Los Cabos in Baja California.

Over the years I had made many, many costumes for my handsome American grandchildren, mostly for Halloween. Everything from Peter Pan, Tinker Bell and Captain Hook to Mary Poppins and year after year they won prizes for the best costume.

Michael's Family

Michael has three children, a daughter, Lucinda, and two sons, Silas and Simeon, aged 48, 46 and 42, (in 2005) and now three grandchildren, Manon, Jade and Zak. Since then Sim has had another son, born in 2007 and called Ty Kane. They live with Simeon's fiancé in Holland at the moment.

The amazing thing is that our four sons names all begin with 's', so we have Si, Si, Sim and Sean and Lucinda who is usually called Cin. Michael's second name is Hyde, the same as my former sister-in-law, Janice, and his first wife was a Miss Potter, a family name of mine.

About two years after I moved to Cheshire Simeon celebrated his twenty-first birthday. We decided to make it a theme party, but the only theme we could agree upon was 'out of the grave'! Almost everyone dressed up. We had corpses, mourners, a mummy, and ghosts. Sean was over from California at the time and he said the only things he thought came out of a grave were maggots. So I made him a maggot costume! Unfortunately I cut the hole for the neck in the wrong place and when Sean put it on he looked hunchbacked. Before the party began, he and the rest of the lads retired to the Bull's Head pub near the top of our drive and by the time Sean came back he was a 'drunken hunchbacked maggot'!

Cin married first, a Frenchman, Alain Brillant, who was awful. Actually he was a very attractive to look at and was a talented graphic designer but he was an alcoholic lazy man. Cin met him when they both worked for a Parisian design and packaging firm. They married in June, 1988 in England, but returned to live in Paris. Cin became pregnant very quickly and nine moths after the wedding Manon arrived on March 2nd 1989. Because Cin and Alain were living in Paris we bought a holiday home just north of Chablis so that they could use it for weekends. The marriage lasted less than three years before we were forced to go to France to bring Cin and Manon home. They lived in Wilmslow for a while before moving nearer to Macclesfield. After a nervous break down Cin found it difficult to cope with a small child and so Manon came to live with us.

Simeon began a relationship with Angie Clewes and their daughter Jade was born on August 8th 1989. She and Manon are first cousins but as different as chalk and cheese. Manon is very dark haired with grey eyes, while Jade is platinum blond and although she is very intelligent you would think, to listen to her, that she is the typical 'dizzy blond' because she never stops giggling.

Sim and Angie's delightful son Zak arrived on September 8th 1993. Zak is very much into playing sport, including rugby, football and cricket.

Silas has never married – so far anyway.

Lucinda

Lucinda (Cin) has never fully recovered since her marriage to Alain and is very reluctant to allow anyone into her house. It is so sad as she is an artistic and intelligent woman, but one who has wasted so much of her life. For a while she taught design and packaging on a part-time basis at Blackpool College of Art, but when the funding became tight she lost the hours she was working. Since then she has done very little, although she is now doing some French conversation coaching with the fifteen year old daughter of a friend of hers.

Silas

When I first met Si he was running a restaurant and bed and breakfast business in Orton, near Penrith. He later moved to Oswestry, where he started another restaurant. He never seemed to have a shortage of girlfriends but none of them attracted him enough to want to either marry, or have children. In fact he never seemed to have a lot in common with any of his girlfriends over the years.

Becoming fed up with restaurant hours, which did not allow him to have a proper social life he sold out and took on a business which took him around golf clubs and similar shops. Then two years ago, in 2007 he bought a Reeds Rains franchise and became an Estate Agent. It was this move that actually took me back into training Estate Agents again, when I rejoined Reeds Rains as a very part-time trainer.

Simeon

He has had the most varied life of the three. Since I have known him he has owned his own Estate Agency business, the re-building and refurbishment of properties, in the U.K., Holland, France and now in Germany. He has lived in all four countries and also Tenerife.

Simeon has a great sense of humour, while sometimes a bit weird, as demonstrated with his relationship with Sean. In many ways *they* are more like brothers than with their own siblings.

One of my early memories of Sim was of him borrowing my mascara and eye liner. It was the 'Romantics' period of fashion for men. When I asked him what he would like for his birthday, he told me blue mascara! His children think it is very funny to believe that their father wore 'make-up'.

It was the girls who got Michael and I muddled – there were so *many* of them and I am sure we called them by the wrong name on many occasion, not having realised that she was past news.

There was a stage when Sim was working as a barman at a pub in Macclesfield. He thought Simeon was a bit 'posh' for this particular down at heel establishment close to the football ground and so he called himself 'John'. Only problem was that he didn't respond when someone shouted 'John' as he had forgotten his new name. Many a punter accused him of either ignoring them or of deafness.

He has now completely settled down, is the very proud father of his third child, Ty and has become a house-dad. I don't think he realised how hard it is to bring up a toddler!

Michael's Elder Brother, Peter

Peter was Michael's elder brother and then younger than him are Margaret, and his brother Tim who was the youngest by a number of years.

Peter was always my favourite. He was a very knowledgeable bee keeper with anything up to forty hives spread around in peoples gardens and up on the Derbyshire moors. He often came to visit and tell us his latest adventures. – he also told me naughty stories and jokes. Many at time we sat in our kitchen and screamed with laughter.

I recall one day when he arrived and was feeling a bit sorry for himself. The day before he'd had a swarm of bees in his garden. Rushing out with a swarm box he'd succeeded in capturing the queen and her entourage. Pete left the box on a post for the other bees to join the colony. Later that night, as he was about to climb into bed, Pete remembered the swarm and knowing that if he didn't get it into a hive that night they would have flown away by the morning. Hurrying, he pulled on his trousers and while transferring the bees he suddenly got stung where no beekeeper should ever get stung! He had forgotten to zip his trousers up! His unmerciful brother, Michael, just said, "Did it swell up a lot Pete?"

At that time we had several dozen hens and a number of ducks and Peter became very interested in them. Actually one of the most unnerving things in my life happened with our big Muscovy drake. I took, what I thought was, an almost empty bag of corn out to feed the birds. As I tipped the remains out, a big fat, well fed, live mouse landed at my feet, but before I could do anything the drake grabbed it and *swallowed it whole*. I didn't know what to do but I could hear the poor creature squeaking all the way down the drake's throat! I sort of stood there going, 'Oh! Oh! Oh!'

Peter, Michael and I toyed with the idea of raising lots of free range hens on our big field at Brook House Farm. Pete managed to find some old rabbit houses which he bought and which he thought might make great chicken houses. He began to read poultry world and saw an article about a very large poultry convention in Atlanta in the States. He decided to attend it. He signed up and was told to meet other delegates at Manchester Airport. When he arrived at 'check-in' everybody else seemed to know each other and were busily discussing their flocks.

"How many hens have you got?"

"Half a million now," responded one.

"I've only got just over a quarter of a million," said another.

"I'm up to one hundred and sixty five thousand," and so on until one of them politely asked Pete how many he'd got.

"Thirty six," Pete replied.

"Thirty six thousand?

"No. Thirty six hens."

The delegates looked at him and at each other in total astonishment.

Peter often came on holidays with Michael and me. He travelled with us several times to France, once to Australia and a couple of times to California. He was always excellent company. When he was in his late seventies, he decided to see how fast he could get his Volvo to go. "I had it up to 126 m.p.h. on the auto route from Calais," he cheerfully told us.

He died, a few days after his eightieth birthday, from a brain tumour.

I often think about him and the times he came and sat at our kitchen table drinking coffee and talking about his precious bees.

Tim

Michael's younger brother, Tim, I didn't know well as well as Pete and Margaret, although he was another of the Reeds Rains partners. Tim died, like Peter of a brain tumour. He was quieter than Michael or Pete, except for the odd evening at the 'Thieves Neck' pub in Woodford, so I understand. He was very proud of both his sons who are very clever. Nicholas, who is exactly one year older than Simon, is an amazing photographer and now lives in Brisbane, Australia with his wife Jonelle plus a variety of pets. Jonelle rescues baby possums and brings them on so they can be released back into the wild. They have had the odd problem when huge snakes have raided the cages and the possums were no longer there in the morning – just a very fat sleepy snake.

Jonathan is a surveyor specialising in sorting out problems with water, like pumping water from area to area. He has just received his doctorate. His wife, Gaynor is an accountant and they have two children, Michael and Freya.

Margaret

Michael's sister Margaret, who is four years younger than him, has had a sad life suffering from mental ill health. She never married, although she was engaged in her late teens. She was fine until after she left Athol Crescent, The Edinburgh College of Domestic Science and returned home when her ill health began and has continued throughout her life. When she is well she is very kind, but can change quickly under stress.

Anthony

Anthony came into my life a long time after I arrived in Cheshire. He is a wonderful character who has been a wheelwright for much of his life. Anthony has led almost a gypsy life, travelling round the horse fairs and meeting many unusual people in the course of his work. After a recent fall, when he broke his hip, we went to his house in Derbyshire. Everything in it is in a sort of a time warp. Apart from finding carriage wheels and horse harnesses and other gear in every room, including his bedroom, nothing has been changed for probably forty or more years. Almost everything has been allowed to deteriorate to such an extent that he is currently in sheltered accommodation

Sales and Motivation Training

After moving to Cheshire I continued with my training for Estate Agents. To begin with I worked with lots of different firms before joining Reed Rains as their sales trainer. Later, after Michael and his partners had sold the firm to the Prudential, I stayed on as Training Officer for the North West. I became very unhappy with the Prudential when they expected me to teach 'hard sell' tactics and resigned not long before Michael retired.

In 2007 I returned to training for Reeds Rains on a very part-time basis, but still working in the way I have always done. No overhead projectors or power points, just the class sitting round a table and working together as a group.

Stockport County and Danny Bergara

Although, after I left the Prudential, I did some Estate Agency work, I went on with my Goal Setting and Motivation classes. The classic time was with the footballers of Stockport County Football Club of which Michael became a Director in about 1987. Danny Bergara, who was probably the best Manager the Club has ever had, was very keen on motivation. While I was down at the Club one afternoon he asked me if I would give the players a pep talk.

"But I don't have my notes with me," I told Danny.

"That's all right," he said in his Uruguayan accent, "They've all come in from training and they are in the bath right now," he said. "You stay in my office and then come down to the dressing room in about ten minutes."

I don't who was more scared, them or me! There were twenty six young men with towels wrapped round them. I harangued them for thirty one minutes – and at the end of the season we had gone from the bottom of the division to almost the top and played at Wembley in a lower league division Cup Final match. Two of the young men came and told me they hadn't appreciated my talk until later on in the season. At the end of the season they came and said thank you. We went on to gain promotion the following year and again the year after that. It was only when Danny left that later managers would not allow me to do the pre-season pep talk. Strange –Stockport dropped back down to the bottom division! However in 2009, one of the former players is now the manager and we are back in Division 1 so perhaps he remembered my words.

It was at a Stockport County match Manon uttered a classic remark. One of the other director's wives really could pack back the white wine. On a very cold afternoon she decided to remain in the Board Room after half time and proceeded to prop up the bar. On our way home Manon, who was about seven at the time, remarked, "She's very nice isn't she, that mad drunk woman!" How right she was – especially the mad, drunk bit!

East Cheshire Hospice

Both Michael and I were involved in fund raising for the local Hospice. He became head of the first main fund raising committee and later I was a Trustee. During this time I was asked to head up the 10th Anniversary Appeal. We were challenged to raise £300,000 in one year. It took us one and a half years.

One of our efforts involved a breakfast in a marquee in the, very brief, presence of HRH The Princess Royal. After a bit of a skirmish with a couple of people at the Hospice, we invited local business men who we thought would give us lots of money. We asked if Her Royal Highness would say a few words and were told no. Then my committee told me I would have to speak. Looking back I am not sure I would have done it if it had been now, although looking at my family tree, I reckon my background is as good as hers.

I was introduced to her, and immediately asked whether I could say a few words. Poor woman, before Her Royal Highness had time to say no, I jumped in with my two minute speech. I still have the photographs of her looking very elegant but with a frozen look on her face! It did work however and she very graciously spoke to quite a few people there who did cough up some of the money we needed.

I am still fund raising for the Hospice. We hold a bi-annual Art Fair which is becoming more and more prestigious. We have successfully launched the careers of some fine artists.

At the time of writing I am recovering from a Cookery Demonstration. Opening my big mouth as usual I blithely announced at someone else's rather ponderous demo that I could produce ten dishes in one hour. However on this occasion I actually cooked eleven dishes in just over one hour. Three starters, four main courses and four desserts were on my list. Might have been a big mistake! It looks as though I will be expected to repeat the effort.

Between us, my husband and I, raised a lot of money and were invited to Buckingham Palace to a garden party held by the Queen. It was a fascinating day. I was also invited to attend a lunch, as a prospective winner of Cheshire woman of the Year, another honour.

I did not win; I hasten to add, because there were a great many more deserving women there at the lunch.

Prestbury Village Youth Groups Pantomime

This became a large part of my life for a while. I made, and still do after twenty two years, costumes for the pantomimes. I directed it for four years; did two years on lighting and four years as stage director and only packed it in because Michael was getting fed up with the amount of commitment I had to put in. The pantomime was very hard work with one year running into the next. The kids aged eleven to eighteen could be very difficult to handle, especially after the first few weeks when they became bored if they only had small parts. I even added in four more Merry Men for Babes in the Wood, starring Robin Hood, when we had extra girls who wanted to be in it. That year we had fifty-one teenagers taking part.

Fortune Telling

Over the years I have continued to read the cards and hands and do believe I have become stronger in my abilities, particularly with the hands. I do not know what the lines mean and so I generally just close my eyes and allow pictures to come into my mind. I have many, many examples of *pictures* I have *seen,* but will only mention a couple. Every year to do readings at the Hospice annual summer fete. I try to avoid telling people about death or divorce – because I can always be wrong.

I have had several of, what I call, watery deaths. The first happened when I was staying with Jennie Farrant. We had been to an Old School Reunion in 2001. I was fifty-nine at the time and hadn't been back to Rye Grammar School since I left in 1957. What a shock it was! They were all old! I couldn't believe seeing all those old people! I'll never go again. Anyway, Jennie asked me to stay and invited some other people to join us for dinner. One couple had recently returned from the States where the husband had been sent by his newspaper to investigate the paranormal and Para psychological. It was only after the readings that Jenny told me this.

While doing the hand reading it was as if I was watching someone drowning. It was awful. The whole experience was as if I was seeing it happen right in front of me – in moving colour. I *watched* an arm come out of a grey, rough sea which I described as being like the Irish Sea, but I didn't think it was the Irish Sea. The arm disappeared and I knew someone had drowned. When I had finished the man told me that nobody in the house knew this story and he hadn't thought about it for years. I was wrong about the Irish Sea because it did happen there. A friend of his father's had been making a crossing between Scotland and Ireland when he was washed overboard from the yacht he was on and had drowned.

Another 'watery death', and I have had several others, occurred when I was invited to go to an old lady's house in Macclesfield – she said she thought her mother wanted to come through. During the reading everything in my mind went black with just a red glow in the centre and then suddenly I couldn't breathe. I found myself gasping. When I'd recovered my breath, I asked the old lady whether she had lost anyone during the war. Someone who was drowned at sea – possibly an uncle or cousin. She said no, she didn't know who it might be. I persisted but she couldn't think of anyone. I left, but next morning she phoned and said it had come to her during the night. A cousin of hers had been in a submarine when it was sunk by the Germans. That was it. That was the reason I couldn't breathe – I believe he suffocated to death! The darkness with just the red glow could have been the emergency lights.

The Ghost of Mr Bowler

It became apparent after a while that we were not alone in the farmhouse. Manon, our part French grand daughter was staying with us and, at the age of about two and a half, woke up crying one night. She repeatedly said she'd seen a face. At the time I thought it was a

189

reflection of the moon shining on the mirror, until I worked out it was impossible for the moon to cause Manon to cry out. It took us a long time to get her back to sleep.

On another occasion, when Simon was visiting us, I found him asleep downstairs. Upon questioning him as to why he'd come down during the night, he explained that he could not sleep in the spare bedroom because there was something very odd and frightening about it. This was not the same room Manon had slept in.

Then one January night in 1990 I woke up to find a man in the bedroom. I was naturally terrified thinking it was an intruder who would probably murder us. While panicking and wondering how he'd entered the house because the burglar alarm was activated downstairs, I realised I was looking at an old man sitting beside the bed. He had a very ruddy complexion, as though he'd spent a lot of time out in all kinds of weather, and deep lines chiselled from his nose to the sides of his mouth. Staring straight at me, with what I thought were steel grey eyes, I felt that his face, which was very clear, was lit by either candle or an old fashioned oil lamp. I lay there staring back at him wishing I could draw. He remained completely in focus until I moved, at which point he began to fade away. His features became fuzzier and fainter until he totally disappeared and the room was pitch black again. It was probably only a matter of seconds before he was gone but it was a definite fading rather than an instantaneous disappearance. Wide awake I tried to imprint his face in my memory.

A few days later I submitted a description of my ghostly sighting to the village magazine and within twelve hours of it being distributed, four different older ladies telephoned me and said that it must have been the ghost of *Mr Bowler*, I had described him exactly. The old ladies had known him when they were children. One of them even told me he had given her lifts to Alderley Edge on his milk wagon as he took his churns to catch the train into Manchester. I was wrong about his eyes, they were in fact blue but he frightened these children because he had a habit of staring at them. One of the ladies asked me if he was wearing a hat. I could only say that I had got an impression of a sort of trilby shape.

He had lived at Brook House Farm from about 1910 until about

1930, but the strangest thing wasn't he didn't die there, he moved at least twice. Why he was haunting us we have no idea.

Then a most extraordinary thing happened. In 2003, I was sitting outside the house on a glorious summer morning having a cup of coffee, when a man drove into the central yard. He asked me if our house, Brook House Farm, had appeared on television the previous evening. I assured him, that as far as I knew, it hadn't. He insisted his mother had been talking on the telephone when she caught a glimpse of the Farm and had recognised it. I again repeated that I was unaware of it being televised. He then went on to tell me his mother had convalesced at the Farm seventy years earlier when she came to stay with her Uncle and Aunt Bowler. I remember being struck dumb for a moment before telling him that her *Uncle Bowler* was our ghost. When he explained that his mother did not live with he and his wife, but did come to stay with them, I invited him to bring her for coffee the next time she was visiting.

Sure enough a few weeks later John, the son of Mr Bowler's niece, phoned and I invited the three of them to come and see us. He told me he had said very little to her.

They arrived and I asked the old lady if she would like to see the house before we had coffee. She accepted. Downstairs had changed quite a bit but upstairs was still very similar. One room, the bedroom my son Simon hated, she pointed out was her aunt's storeroom for jam and chutney. Another room she recalled as being her bedroom, but when I took her into our bedroom and the scene of the haunting, she pointed to one corner and said she remembered this room as her aunt and uncle's bedroom, she added that he'd had a small round table in the corner where he kept his cream and medication – the poor man suffered from severe arthritis, and there had been a chair right beside it. My jaw dropped in astonishment because that was *exactly* where I had seen the ghost sitting. I then described my experience and she confirmed that she was sure I had seen her uncle. When I told her about the hat, she said he always wore a battered trilby because, in those days, he milked his cows by hand and he used to lean his head up against their thighs. John then produced a photograph of his Great Uncle Bowler and there he was with the hat.

I did say that it is not everyday when one meets the relative of a ghost!

Our ghost was around for many years. One day when Manon and I were in the kitchen immediately below the hated bedroom, we both heard footsteps above us. Manon immediately said she thought Granddad was out but she'd just heard him in his study overhead. I agreed he was out but was a little worried that someone might have broken into the house. I locked the door leading off the hall and into the part we were in. Then I went outside and looked around. There was nothing there – no doors or windows open, nothing. It had to be Mr Bowler we had both heard so clearly.

Mr Bowler has now disappeared. We no longer heard his footsteps in 'Simon's' room and the very heavy front door knocker didn't bang any more – he has gone, courtesy of my friend Anne Mitchell. Anne is an extraordinary acupuncturist, healer - and remover of ghosts. When I realised Mr Bowler was no longer around, I asked Anne if she had sent him on his way.

"Didn't you want me to?"

"No." I replied.

"Well I'm afraid he's gone. He was earth bound, I have sent him to the light, he is much happier now."

Church or a Chapel?

It was around the same time I had a vivid dream. I dreamt that in our field behind the house there were stone walls, about a metre high, of a ruined church or chapel. It was so clear in my mind I went into the field the next morning to see if I could see anything. The only indication there might be something there was a slight indentation in the ground. However, Michael said he thought it had been trodden down when the cattle had gathered round a water trough.

A few years later in the field in front of us, about one hundred metres away from the place in my dream, a horse died. A young man came with a large mechanical digger to dig a hole to bury it. He went down about a metre and a half and came across stone walls. Digging a further metre or so he discovered huge timber beams and loose stone flooring. He'd found a medieval building. Unfortunately, as the owner of the horse was so anxious to get it buried, they wouldn't let him dig another pit further away.

The young man's mother and I discussed the use of the building, she thought it was probably an old mill because it is near a stream, but I couldn't get the dream out of my head and insisted it was a church or a chapel. One odd thing about this building it that the stone floor is two meters below the lowest level of the stream! Only six meters away!

Then I realised we live on Priest Lane. Why? There is one little church in the village and that was only built 100 years ago. Why was it called Priest Lane? Our village is Mottram St Andrew, also with a religious connotation.

Later, when talking to an American friend who uses dousing rods, I mentioned the building. Stopping me quickly she told me not to say any more but asked if I had a map of the area so she could douse over that and tell me what, if anything, she could find. Christiane, my friend, came back to me and said she'd picked up the impression that a church or chapel had been destroyed about thirteen hundred. This matched my dream, however the site was in neither of the two places I knew about, but was actually higher up the slope, near the ancient Saxon Cross which is beside the main road.

I invited Christiane to come and see me and we first made our way to where my dream indicated the building. Both of us carried dousing rods - it was my first try at using them, and as we slowly made our way side by side, our rods suddenly swung and crossed at precisely the same moment. Christiane confirmed there was a building below the ground. She was not very comfortable with the feeling and thought it might have been a plague house where many people had died.

Making our way to where I knew the medieval building was, with the dead horse on top, Christiane very quickly discovered the exact site. It was rather larger than the bit we had found earlier and in fact was 'L' shaped. This building had housed monks or nuns she thought.

On another occasion, Anne Mitchell visited me and, without telling her Christiane's thoughts, we went through the same routine. The findings were exactly the same. Anne even saying she thought the church had been destroyed by a lightening strike in 1304.

We haven't dug down to find out what might be there but perhaps someone like the Time Team could investigate it one day.

Since then, Christiane and I were given permission to go into the garden and with dousing rods we began to search the area. We think we found the sites of not one but three churches, the earliest dating back to Saxon times. We both doused to see how deep it was. I thought about eight feet and Christiane came up with seven and a half feet. Then Christiane decided to see if she could find the corners of another 'church'. Struggling between trees and undergrowth she walked until she 'found' each corner. When we looked at it afterwards she had marked out a perfect rectangle.

Dame Felicitas

Following on from Churches and chapels brings back memories of Dame Felicitas Corrigan of Stanbrook Abbey, in Worcestershire, who died in 2003. Stanbrook is a Benedictine Abbey and an enclosed order. Although most of the nuns never leave Stanbrook, they do have others who go to places like Nigeria to work with the poor and sick.

Dame Felicitas was one month younger than mother and had the same extraordinary brain. Mother first came across Dame Felicitas when my sister had, the doctors said, an incurable blood disease. One afternoon, when mother was listening to the radio, she heard a programme about Stanbrook. In desperation she wrote and asked them to pray for Jo. Two days later, Jo suddenly said she felt a bit better and when she next visited the hospital they were astonished to find nothing wrong with her!

Over the years I have written and have told other people to write to the nuns of Stanbrook and many miracles have occurred after the nuns have prayed, but it was Dame Felicitas we became close to. It was when I moved to Cheshire that I undertook the typing of several of her books for publication. One of them, a history of the early Benedictines, was horrendous to work on as a great deal of the language was medieval English. But doing this was one way of saying thank you.

Dame Felicitas used to send out regular newsletters and my favourite began: *Paddy O'Flaherty's whisky is in short supply at Stanbrook. As one guest said – 'It flows down the gullet as smoothly as a choir singing hymns all the way'.* And this from a nun who had been living, almost entirely, behind the high walls of the Abbey for seventy years.

Another lovely story connected with Dame Felicitas. She wrote the original book which was then turned into the play, 'The Best of Friends' about Dame Laurentia McLachlan, former Abbess of Stanbrook, George Bernard Shaw and Sir Sydney Cockerell, played by John Gielgud. In real life the three of them wrote and communicated for many years, maintaining a sort of intellectual love/hate relationship.

The story in the play, which I particularly enjoyed, was about an elderly aunt who died overseas. The family arranged for her coffin to be sent back to England for burial. Upon arrival it was discovered the wrong coffin had been forwarded and the one which arrived contained the body of a Russian General. The family notified the Russian Embassy and in due course received the reply. 'Do what you like with the General. Your aunt has been buried with full military honours!'

CHAPTER 17
WHISTLER AND DIANA

Christmas and New Year 2001

In the year 2001 we were invited to join Joe and Diana for Christmas and New Year in Whistler, near Vancouver in Canada. They had 'acquired' a large house right on the edge of a beautiful lake. When we arrived the lake was completely frozen over and the snow several feet deep. It was quite beautiful. They had a hot tub outside on their patio and one afternoon/evening, we took our cocktails with us, and climbed into the hot water to enjoy the snowy scene all round us.

Diana had gone overboard, as she did every year, with her Christmas decorations. She had an artificial tree, twenty feet tall, with about 1000 tiny bulbs permanently on it. Diana always had help to decorate her home for the holidays. It took two of them nearly a week to put everything up and she began immediately after Thanksgiving at the end of November. This year was no exception in the decorating, but, as she wanted other people to see her house, she didn't take the decorations down until the end of February!

She was behaving a little oddly, and one day, she preferred to go off with Joe to have her nails painted a particularly virulent sea green, leaving Michael and I to fend for ourselves. There was no question about us going with them. We did that by taking the bus into Whistler to walk around the delightful ski town. Thinking it was rude to stay out too long, we made our way back to the house mid afternoon, only to find our hosts still out – they didn't get back until well after 6.00pm, because they had decided to go out for lunch!

Her niece, 26 year old Deanna, arrived on Christmas Eve and Diana was all over her. She was even talking about adopting her and cutting their children out of their Wills. This didn't last for long as they fell out about a year later.

Christmas Day was interesting, but my overwhelming memories are of eating too much stodgy and over sweet food. Sweet potatoes with marshmallows were one of her specialities. I think the most un-thought about gift was the enormous musical, turning snow scene which weighed a ton and which we had to cart back on the plane. It was OK, but when she said she had given an identical thing to her cleaning lady, I felt, as close friends, we should have ranked a little bit higher!

Boxing Day

Canada does celebrate Boxing Day, although the United States doesn't. We had arranged to drive into Vancouver to visit the huge indoor Boxing Day market. Leaving much later than we originally decided we set off. This was because Diana could not decide which of her fur coats she should wear. She lent her Russian fur to Deanna and then tried on one fur after another. Should it be the black mink, or the golden mink or whatever else she had in her wardrobe?

In the end she chose her ocelot trimmed with black mink with a matching hat that looked like a Mountie's. Ocelot is a spotted fur. Underneath she was dressed all in black, with very heavy makeup, her blue/green nails, and her jet black hair (not her normal colour) tied back in a pony tail we finally set off. I have to say here that I was wearing a Marks and Spencer beige coloured wool coat – not really in the same class as the other two.

The road to Vancouver was hedged by large snow drifts on either side. It wasn't long before Deanna, who was sitting in the very back of their 4 x 4 vehicle, began to feel car sick, something she regularly suffered from. I tried to persuade Diana to switch places, but no, she wouldn't. In the end, after a not too reasonable discussion, I moved right to the back, Joe sat in my place beside Michael, while Diana stayed exactly where she'd been sitting and they let Deanna, who had never driven a high powered vehicle like theirs before, drive us into

Vancouver – over snowy and icy roads. I can tell you I was scared to death! This wasn't the first example of Diana's selfishness but the most prominent I had come across at that time.

The Market

Diana loves to have her photograph taken and after one photo shoot stop en route we continued on to Vancouver and the fabulous market. Once there we drifted around, Joe taking photos of them as they, in their expensive fur coats, posed beside stalls piled high with cheeses and gifts. I, in my Marks and Spencer beige didn't come into it – and then I noticed a Canadian family, both husband and wife very tall. He was pushing a buggy with a little girl in it, while his wife walked along holding a little boy's hand. Suddenly the mother pointed to Diana and said to the child, "Look, there's Cruella DeVille!" – And she was right. Diana didn't hear the remark and I have never told her.

New Year's Eve

This has got to be the most expensive evening we have had or will ever have again. At £300 a head it had to be spectacular. Diana and Deanna began preparing themselves at around 2.00pm, as she did on the Alaskan cruise. Dressed in our finery we headed for Chateau Whistler at about 7.00pm. Joe had been to collect our 'tickets' earlier. These were bags of blue water with our names on. The theme that night was the sea.

Upon arrival we were met by beautifully dressed mermaids and other 'human' sea creatures. Inside the huge ballroom, colours rippled off the walls as if we were under the sea and sounds of dolphins and whales echoed round us. Later, stilt walking people fabulously dressed as fish moved through the room.

Our table was for ten and so five strangers were due to join us. Michael and I were quite prepared to wait for them to arrive and in fact Michael was about to order the wine, when our three hosts got up to choose their starters from the most amazing buffet of hot and cold foods. There was every type of fish and meat and salads and hot food you could possibly think of, followed by dozens of wonderful puddings.

We remained at the table, because by now, two of the other guests had arrived. Diana, Deanna and Joe came back with piled plates, half of which Diana and Deanna left, and without even acknowledging the new comers, proceeded to scoff away. Deanna, by the way, was still wearing her coat, not because it was cold, but because her dress was too tight after the Christmas festivities.

They then leapt up again to go for their main courses still leaving us sitting there. The other three people arrived. The wife was a little strange and kept dashing off to talk to strangers at other tables. However her husband told us she had been diagnosed with terminal cancer and he wanted her just to enjoy herself that evening.

By the time we and the others were ready to hit the buffet, our friends were already on their desserts. After that they sat there, barely talking to anyone except themselves, while we had a great evening.

The cabaret was fantastic and so was the music and at midnight a 'waterfall' of silver streamers descended from the ceiling.

Not ready to give up, the five of us wandered into a 'pub' filled with young people from all over the world. Michael and I joined them, while the other three sat in a corner in stony silence. They certainly didn't get much for their money unlike Michael and me.

In many ways it was a blessed relief to climb on to the plane, clutching the heavy snow scene, to fly home.

Diana – June 2007

Joe called me in mid June to tell me that Diana had shot herself. To begin with we couldn't work out whether it was an accident or a suicide attempt, or a deliberate attempt to implicate either Joe or Sherrie, who was living with them at the time. Still don't know, but she was found, having nearly bled to death because she had shot herself through her right hip and into her left thigh. By this stage she was really swinging from highs to almost complete depression and was totally irrational and while in hospital, poor woman, she fell off the hospital trolley and broke her leg. Part of the problem may have been her extreme thinness. Diana was an American size 0 or 1. Some months later she was diagnosed with cancer and has since been through chemotherapy, which seems to have done the trick.

She and Joe have moved several times since returning from Canada. While house hunting they lived in a hotel for about a year.

Diana is obsessed with her appearance and with Channel clothes and jewellery, much to Joe's chagrin.

Diana's family

Over the years I have learnt more about Diana's family, often from her very long letters one of which reached eighty pages. In that one she explained that her father had attempted to arrange her mother's cremation eight times before her mother even became ill and died. Her father told Diana that he had given her something to make her die. It was six months after her mother's death when she found out about it. She received a letter from her father saying that he knew Diana always wanted to be with her mother and so he had arranged to have her ashes scattered from an airplane over Diana and Joe's house.

She now has no communication with any of her children or grandchildren. The children won't let her near them. There are so many other strange and sad stories connected with her, that it is understandable she has such a dysfunctional family.

CHAPTER 18
AN UPDATE ON OUR LIVES

Manon

Manon has been with us for about thirteen years now and has grown up into a beautiful young woman now aged twenty. Talented, funny and a great golfer, she is popular with both boys and girls. I think she takes after her grandfather because most of the time she is a very kind girl. Manon writes well and takes part in many sports. I do keep telling her not to *always* win whenever she takes on the boys at snooker, golf, tennis, table tennis or other sports because boys do like to win!

When she first left school she attended college, where she studied Sports Science, getting distinctions in every subject. She is now at University in Sheffield doing Property Development and Estate Management, although she is considering returning to doing a degree in Sports.

We have moved again!

Only three hundred yards but I think it is the most stressful move I have ever made, and this had a ghost as well! I realised within two weeks of moving that there was a presence in the cottage, and this one wasn't benign like Mr Bowler, but nasty. He didn't approve of us or the changes we were making.

I phoned Anne Mitchell again to ask for help and she has sent him on his way – thank goodness because I think he was trying to frighten us.

Built in about 1800, the cottage was originally two tiny dark worker's cottages. New windows, one part of the roof raised and, we hope, it will feel like home in the not too distant future. Certainly Manon's rooms are futuristic with fake leopard and tiger skin covers on sofa and bed.

Libby

Libby met and married a delightful man called Nic Castle. They now have a very bright and pretty baby daughter, Georgie, born on 14th October 2007.

Nic and Libby married in October 2006 in a castle in Cheshire. During the reception one very curious thing happened. Rob my nephew, Manon and I decided to go and have a drink while photos were being taken. The three of us were walking along a long wide corridor when both Manon and Rob both called out at the same time – "Did you see that?" I didn't because I was looking at the pictures on one wall and they had both been facing the other way. As we approached a large fireplace, they had seen a heavy brass fire screen rock backwards and forwards, but there was nobody around – just the three of us. Rob went over to see if it could have been blown by a draft, but it was almost too heavy to lift – but they both saw it move.

My sister Jo also told us she had heard heavy footsteps going up and down the corridor outside her bedroom throughout the night. The sounds were confirmed by several other guests.

Jo

My sister moved into sheltered accommodation in Alderley Edge in 2006 and we were working on writing and recording a series of CDs for Estate Agents. Not realising she had cancer, she was admitted into hospital on 9th October, was moved to the Hospice a week later, where she died on October 21st 2008.

Holidays in South Africa and Chile

We were lucky enough to have two wonderful holidays in South Africa and Chile. We went to South Africa to follow the English cricket team and to taste some of their wines. The two memories that stand out most in my mind are the day/night match in Capetown. As the darkness came down, so did the temperatures. I can't remember ever feeling so cold as we sat high up on the terraces. Along with other British visitors who were also there for the cricket, none of us guessed the temperature could change so much.

The other was a three night trip to Shamwari Game Reserve. Driven in an open Land Rover by a charming young Zulu man, we saw almost all of the 'Big Five' animals, including a black rhino that hadn't been seen for weeks and a leopard, another rare sight. It was a magical visit. The hotel was of the highest standard and the food excellent.

We visited Chile on a wine tasting tour. It was fabulous. Starting in Santiago, we tasted at several old and delightful vineyards. Then it was a two night trip further north to Valparaiso and a visit, via a very rickety cable car, to the English settlement high above the harbour, followed by a short drive further where we staying in a wonderful hotel quite literally almost touching the Pacific Ocean.

After several more excursions, we were driven over the Andes and down into Argentina. Twenty eight consecutive hairpin bends took us up to the top of the pass, before the far gentler journey into Argentina. Only one thing almost marred the trip was when the Argentine customs people decided we needed to get our entire tightly crammed in luggage out of the van for them to check, however a quick exchange of a $10 bill between Sue, our leader, and the customs man saw us quickly on our way!

We infinitely preferred Chile to Argentina, however the old town of Mendoza was worth the visit, especially the evening meal we consumed. There were eleven of us who visited one of the best restaurants in the city. We all had pre-dinner drinks, starters, fillet steaks, loads of wine, water, coffee and petit fours and the total bill for all of us, and including the tip, came to £120!

One day, when staying in Buenos Aires we took a fascinating tour of an area which must be very similar to the Everglades. The boat took us round islands, through channels, and past delightful wooden houses. There are no roads and so everything has to be moved by water.

But the piece de resistance was the Tango lesson Sue organised. Only the ladies went because all the men chickened out. They missed a treat. It was so much fun. I will admit I mistook the male dancer as our taxi driver. A short Argentine with an American accent and jeans that were falling off his bottom met us. I was expecting the typical gaucho type - however he and his pretty partner were very good teachers.

One of our Chilean guides said that in Chile there are a lot of very poor people but no extreme poverty and certainly we didn't see any beggars, unlike Argentina where they were everywhere on the streets of Buenos Aires. We are now gearing up to a visit to New Zealand in 2010.

The Future

My immediate goal is to complete my two novels currently underway and sell my Estate Agency CDs before we head for New Zealand next January.

For me it is back to Jim Rohn's saying – *Let death find me climbing a new mountain.*

APPENDIX I

(Sent to me by The Royal Scots Museum, Edinburgh Castle, June 2005)

Lieutenant Colonel David Aubrey Callender, CMG

Born: 11 November 1868

Lt. Col. D.A. Callender was appointed 2nd Lieutenant in The Royal Scots on 14th September 1887 and joined the 1st Battalion at York.

Promoted to Lieutenant on 23rd January 1890.

On 7th March 1892 he joined the 2nd Battalion at Malta who were embarking on board the transport ship SS *Avoca* bound for India. According to entries in the newly published Regimental magazine *The Thistle*, he acquitted himself well in the field of training and in the other major pastimes of the garrison town of Wellington, Madras, which were cricket, football and gymkhana.

In March 1893 he returned to the U.K. for a spell of duty at the Regimental Depot at Glencorse, near Penicuik, which was responsible for training new recruits and then sending them to one of the two Regular battalions. He took one such draft to the 1st Battalion at York in October 1893.

APPENDIX II

1st BATTALION, THE ROYAL SCOTS, War Diary

1915

APRIL

1st The Battalion was inspected by the G.O.C. in C. 2nd Army, in Brigade.

2nd Battalion parade. Companies exercised in rushing trenches, parties being told off to reverse parapet, close communicating trenches etc. A & D Coys. Engaged in digging this night, in same area as before.

3rd Companies exercised under O.C. Coys in the attack on trenches.

4th Battalion marched to POPERINGHE at 5.30pm, a distance of about 5 miles, and went into billets there. (Easter Sunday, Parade Service at 11.30am. for C. of S. men).

5th) During this period the Battalion remained,
) resting at POPERINGHE. On 6th April Lt. Col.
) CALLENDER, the Adjutant, and Officers and
) N.C.Os of companies visited the new section of
) trenches about to be taken over in the 8th) neighbourhood of YPRES.

8th The Battalion left POPERINGHE (marching by companies) and halted (for teas) at YPRES. Companies left YPRES for the trenches independently at intervals of 15 mins: 'A' company at 6.30 pm followed by B. C. & D Coys in that order.

The new section of trenches is situated some 4 miles due East of YPRES, astride the MENIN road. The trenches are on the whole good but much work required to be done in the nature of building traverses and parados, improving communication trenches and linking up trenches to form a continuous line.

The enemy's trenches are very close on some portion of our front (within 40 yds), and, at another point, are fully 250 yds distant.

Trenches were occupied by A Coy on the right, B in the centre with 1 platoon C Coy on its left.

Across the MENIN road was C. Coy less 1 platoon. Bn Hd:qrs at first with D. Coy in battalion reserve, in INVERNESS COPSE. These dispositions…. (Pages missing)

MAY 1915

7TH Battalion found party 300 strong (2 reliefs of 150 each) to dig and improve a line of defence through YPRES.

8th Battalion ordered to from part of Composite Brigade with 2 Coys each 2nd Bde Royal Irish Fusiliers and 2nd Brigade Leinster Regt.

Lt. Col. CALLENDER to command composite Brigade with Captain H. E. STANLEY-MURRAY as Staff officer – Command of the battalion devolved upon Major H. F. WINGATE with Capt. J. BURKE as Acting Adjut. Composite Brigade dissolved at 6 p.m. and the battalion proceeded with all speed to the ZOUAVE WOOD (HOOGE); under the command of Lt. Col. CALLENDER.

9th By 2 a.m. the battalion was moved up to SANCTUARY WOOD. At dawn the order came to fall back and occupy the G.H.Q.

line some 2 miles to the West. This was done. The enemy's guns had the range of this line to a nicety, and put in a number of shells.

Casualties this day.

Killed 4 men. Wounded Lt. G.M.V. BIDIE, 25 other ranks.

About 6 p.m. orders were received to proceed to SANCTUARY WOOD. Officers went ahead and inspected trenches held by 2nd GLOUCESTERS, and the battalion took over these trenches before dawn the following day. Disposition of battalion – A & D Coys fire trenches, B & C Coys support trenches.

10th A message came to the effect that all was not well on the left. B Coy was ordered to move to the left in support and to clear up the situation. On arrival it was found that the unit on our left had been driven from one of its trenches by the combined effect of Shells and gas. Seeing the enemy about to occupy the trench in some strength, Captain FARQUHARSON advanced his Company at the double and the enemy fled in disorder. B Coy. Had 1 man wounded. The Company occupied the trench and proceeded to make the flank more secure.

Killed this day :- 2 men.

Wounded this day :- 13 men
(1 since died of wounds).

11th Trenches heavily shelled but with little result. Trenches held A Coy. On the right, D in centre, B on left, C in support. The left Company worked hard.

12th Capt. E. S. FARQUHARSON killed in the trench. Shelling continued intermittently all day.

13th C Coy relieved B Coy in left trench. B returning to support trench.

14th No particular incident to record. During last few nights GLOUCESTERS assisted us in digging retrenchment and also diagonal communicating and fire trench combined from front line to retrenchment. The left Company suffered very little from enfilade fire or snipers, although particularly vulnerable to both.

15th A Quiet day; some shelling. Draft of 79 men from 3rd Bn and 40 rejoined from hospital under Capt. M. HENDERSON and 2/Lt J. E. FINDLAY-HAMILTON (Royal Scots Fusiliers).

16th The draft which arrived yesterday was brought up to the trenches tonight. A further draft of 120 men arrived from 3rd Bn. But was 'diverted' to the 1st Bn on arrival at ROUEN.
No incident to record.
Capt. HENDERSON posted to 'B' Coy and 2 Lt. HAMILTON (attached 1st Royal Scots) also to 'B' Coy.

17th A day without incident beyond the usual daily shell ration, now greatly reduced.

18th This night the Brigade (less 1st and 9th Royal Scots) was relieved by the 3rd Cav. Division, and withdrew to a rest area. The ist and 9th Royal Scots remained in the trenches under orders of the 82nd Infantry Brigade until the night 22nd May.
20th May '15 following officers joined the Battalion –
2/Lts J. B. LUMSDEN, J. D. MILNE, R. B. DEVEREUX, K. C. MOTHERSILL

22nd Battalion relieved by WELCH REGT. And moved back to rest area in the neighbourhood of BUSSEBOOM.
Casualties:- period II.V.15. – 22.V.15.
Killed   – 26 men.
Wounded 72 men.

23rd This afternoon the G.O.C. 2ns Army visited the men informally, and complimented them on the work they had done and the share they had taken in the operations round YPRES during the past month. Lt. Co. CALLENDER, MAJOR WINGATE and certain other Officers having proceeded to England on short leave, the command of the Battalion devolved upon CAPT. HENDERSON.

(Some pages missing)

JUNE (Contd)

14th "out a short route march.
Digging parties were supplied for work under R.E. on new line.

20th Relieved 2nd CAMERONS, moving still further to the left.

22nd LT. COL. CALLENDER assumed temporary command of the 81st Inf. Brig. Battalion remained in trenches until relieved by 2nd CAMERONS 27th June, on which night we retired to billets, less 'B' Coy remaining in reserve.
Trenches were shelled on several occasions without much damage.
On the 25th LT. R.D. CURRIE and 8 men arrived from ROUEN. LT. CURRIE posted to D Coy.
Casualties during the period
Killed 1 man
Died of wounds 3 men
Wounded 2/LT J. HOBBS (since died), 6 men.

28th CAPT. A.F. LUMSDEN and 1 man arrived from England.

29th CAPT. LUMSDEN took over command of A Coy. LT. COL. CALLENDER resumed command of the battalion.
During the morning 2 men were wounded by shell fire in ARMENTIERES. The enemy supply the town with a daily ration of 'hate' and a few casualties sometimes result, often amongst the civil population. The men had a bath and

change of clothing and have provided two digging parties since the 27th.

Wounded – 2 men.

30thD Coy. Relieved B Coy as reserve to 2nd CAMERONS.
Wounded – 1 man.

Honours and awards – D.C.M. No.11112 A/Sgt. ANDERSON H, b Coy for gallant conduct near
HOOGE. d/19.VI.15.

Honours & Awards :- D.C.M.
Under date 12.VI.15. the following appeared in recognition of work done at ST. ELOI (List 33)
9136 C.Q.M.S. BRANNAN T, 'B' Coy
10621. Sgt. HOGG J. 'B' Coy.
7349 A/Cpl. WALLACE T. 'D' Coy
10362 L/Cpl. WILLSON T. 'B' Coy

Mentioned in despatches, dated 31st May for distinguished and gallant conduct in the Field.
LIST G d/22/VI/15.
LT. COL. D.A. CALLENDER.
CAPT. N.S. FARGUS.
LT. N.M. YOUNG.
2 LT J. HOBBS
CAPT. E.J.F. JOHNSTON.
6331 R.Q.M.S. J.D. WILLIAMS.
9545 SCT. CAMPBELL C Coy
9771 L. CPL. SACHS   C Coy
10037 PTE CLARK   A Coy
9972 "   HASTIE   A "

(I have copied these as carefully as possible to the original text.)

APPENDIX III

1ˢᵗ Bn. The Royal Scots

1916 <u>FIELD</u>

Aug.

1ˢᵗBattalion in bivouac at HORTACKOJ.
(They had arrived in SALONIKA, {Thessaloniki} on 13ᵗʰ
February 1916 and spent most of their war in the Struma
Valley fighting against the Bulgarians.)Battalion employed in
erecting sun shelters over bivouacs.

2ⁿᵈBattalion employed on various Brigade fatigues, and in completing
bivouac shelters.

3ʳᵈPhysical Training and hill climbing under Os.C Companies.

4ᵗʰCompany and Squad drill in vicinity of Camp. Lecture to all
officers at Bde Hqrs on Vickars and Lewis Guns.

5ᵗʰ Drill and Attack practise. Lecture by G.O.C. AT Bde Hqrs, to all
OFFICERS, on Trench Warfare.

6ᵗʰ Sunday. Church Parades for all denominations.
<u>6.VIII.16. LEFT BATTN ON COMPLETION OF TOUR OF
DUTY AS COMMANDING OFFICER.</u>
LT. COL. D.A. CALLENDER CMG

7ᵗʰBattalion found various fatigue parties for the Brigade. TOOK
OVER COMMAND OF BATTALION, <u>MAJOR R.R.</u>

FORBES, and 1st A & S. H.

OPERATION ORDER NO. 10.

Operation Order by Lieut. Col. Callender C.M.G.
Comdg. 1ˢᵗ Bn. The Royal Scots.

I.MOVE.

Battalion will move to HORTIACK Tomorrow as under.

Route via AZAMERI.

II.PARADE.

Battalion will parade in present bivouacking area about 0200
    tomorrow. Exact time of parade will be notified later.

III.TRANSPORT.

    All transport, with exception of pack animals will leave at
    1700 today and march via AJVASIL.

IV.BAGGAGE

    All transport to be loaded by 1630 today.

V.INTERVALS AND HALTS.

    As today.

VI.ORDER OF MARCH.

    Hqrs M. G. Section, A.B. Pipers, C.D. Pack Transport.

VII.REAR PARTY.

    O.C. 'D' Coy will detail one Platoon under an Officer to
    march in rear of Pack Transport. He will arrange to off load
    all animals at each hourly.
    29ᵗʰ July 1916

APPENDIX IV

OBITUARY OF
LIEUTENANT COLONEL D.I.H. CALLENDER

(Very kindly prepared by David Murphy, The Royal Scots Regimental Museum)

Hugo was the younger son of Lt. Col. D.A. Callender and was born on 24th March 1913, educated at Radley and the RMC Sandhurst. He was commissioned into The Royal Scots on 2nd February 1933 and joined the 1st Battalion in Aldershot where he soon made a name for himself as a keen boxer and good rugger player and represented the Regiment in both sports.

He joined the 2nd Battalion at Lahore, India in 1935 and moved with them to Hong Kong in January 1938. He left the 2nd Battalion in H.K. at the outbreak of war in 1939 and with a number of Regular officers, returned to the U.K., (the 2nd Bn was lost when the Colony surrendered to the Japanese on 25th December 1941).

I cannot be specific about the next year or so but he probably joined the 1st Battalion in the summer of 1940. The remnants of the Battalion had been reformed at Driffield in East Yorkshire in June 1944 after the majority of the Battalion had been killed or taken prisoner during the rearguard action safeguarding the Dunkirk evacuation. While they returned to full strength the Battalion initially carried out coastal defence duties and assisted the citizens of Hull after bombing raids caused serious casualties and damage to the city.

In April 1942 they sailed from Glasgow for Bombay and after a period of training in India moved up to the Burmese border in December. They fought in the 1st Arakan campaign between March and May 1943, then after a period of organisation in India they were again in action in the Kohima campaign from April 1944.

Hugo served most of the war as a Company Commander, (Major) and was wounded twice during the fighting in Burma.

He was part of the committee responsible for erecting the Battalion's own memorial on the Aradura Spur, Kohima to those that fell during the fighting. The War Memorial was designed and constructed by The Royal Scots themselves under the supervision of a committee composed of Major D.I.H. Callender, the Rev. Crichton Robertson (the Padre) and Captain Tom Dysdale. It was made of local stone and wood, and was erected by the Pioneer Platoon. This monument to the memory of all The Royal Scots who had lost their lives in the Battle of Kohima and the fighting to open the Imphal Road was unveiled by Colonel Masterton Smith on 25th November 1944. The site at Kennedy Hill, on the infamous Aradura Spur, could not have been more appropriate.

After Kohima, the 4th (Infantry) Brigade, including the 1st Battalion, advanced towards Mandalay which took them from January to March 1945. The following moth they returned to India to refit and retrain before going to Malaya in December and it was probably around this point Hugo left the 1st Battalion and was posted to the 7/9th (Highland) Battalion, Royal Scots, a Territorial battalion, at Oldenburg in Germany. He remained with them until their disbandment in June 1946 then joined No. 1 Primary Training Centre & Depot at Glencorse as the Company Commander of the Training Company before taking command of the Training Centre in 1947.

In December 1947 he took over command of C Company, 2nd Battalion in Trieste, an area of tension in the new post-war Europe. Their stay there was fairly uneventful and they returned to Edinburgh at the end of 1948. Prior to the main body returning, new Colours to replace those lost in the Far East after the Japanese invasion and before the merger with the 1st Battalion, were presented by the Colonel-in-Chief, HRH The Princess Royal at Dreghorn Camp, Edinburgh. It was during this ceremony Hugo performed the same duties as his father had carried out at the presentation of the 2nd Battalion's previous Colour in 1911. The two Battalions merged at Dreghorn on 9th February 1949 and at that point Hugo joined the 1st Battalion, The Cameronians, (Scottish Rifles), until he went on to the Nigeria Regiment the following year.

On his return to U.K. he was an instructor at MONS OCS, and then spent the last three years of his service with the Edinburgh University OTC, first as Training Major and then as Commanding Officer.

He retired in November 1958 and for a few years worked with the SSPCA. He was Secretary of the Army Benevolent Fund in Scotland from 1972 until his sudden death on 15th September, 1977.

Hugo will be remembered as a kind, friendly man who was particularly good with the young, a very loyal Royal Scot, who will be greatly missed by all his friends.

APPENDIX V

RICHARD AUBREY CALLENDER

Date of Birth 18th June 1901 in Edinburgh.
Schools: Ascham, Eastbourne; Wellington; Radley

At the time he entered the 2nd Battalion Scots Guards his father, Lt-Colonel D A Callender C.M.G. was living in
6 Grosvenor Crescent, Edinburgh.

He entered Royal Military College, Sandhurst on 1st September 1920

From Royal Military College he was posted to London – 1st February 1923 to be 2nd Lieutenant

To become Lieutenant – 1st February 1925

Resigns his Commission – 8th August 1925

(Note from Lieut.-Colonel Commanding Scots Guards on 31st December 1926)
     This is to certify that Mr. Richard Aubrey Callender served in the Regiment under my command from 1st February 1923 till he resigned his commission on 8th August 1925.
     During that time he was satisfactory both as regards character and as regards the performance of his duties.

To be Lieutenant, retaining his present seniority he joined The Royal Scots – 15th January 1940

21st December 1939 – Note from the War Office
Mr Callender telephoned to say he thought he could get a commission in The Royal Scots and would the Lieutenant-Colonel release him. We told him "Yes".

25th December 1939

Sir,
I am directed to inform you that Lieutenant R. a. Callender, Regular Army Reserve of Officers, Scots Guards, has been ordered to report for duty on 15th January, 1940, to the Officer Commanding, Infantry Training Centre, The Royal Scots, Glencorse Barracks, Edinburgh.
I am,
    Sir,
        Your obedient Servant,

Director of Recruiting and Organisation

Author's Note: We believe he spent the War in training and administration.   At some time he was promoted to the rank of Captain.

APPENDIX VI

WILLIAM ROMAINE CALLENDER MP

(Marble bust of William Romaine Callender can be found in the
main lobby in Manchester Town Hall)

The *Manchester courier,* in its biographical notice of the deceased,
who was the eldest son of the late W.R. Callender Esq., by Hannah,
daughter of Samuel Pope Esq., of Exeter, and was born at Manchester,
in 1825, being consequently in his 51ˢᵗ year, says:-

From early life he took the greatest interest in political matters and
everything which affected the welfare of the working classes. One of the
first matters to which he directed his attention was that of the Factory
Acts, and he was amongst those whom Mr Molesworth in his history
describes as coming forward 'to aid the most helpless and unprotected
classes of society' by putting an end to the overworking of women and
children in mines and factories, for he was not one of those employers
of labour who held that such a limitation would in any way endanger
or destroy their business.

From the time when Sir James Graham, in 1843, introduced his
bill for reducing the hours of labour, and its educational bodies with
the 'Committee of privy Council on Education' (his efforts, however,
proved abortive through the opposition of the Dissenters), Mr Callender
took a deep interest in the Factory Labour question, steadily aided the
agitation for the Ten Hours Bill, which ultimately proved successful,
and in later years he even advocated a limitation of the hours of labour
to nine hours per day, believing that a man would do more work in that
time than if he were compelled to labour for ten hours.

When a very young man, he interested himself in the party politics of the southern division of Lancashire, siding with the Conservatives, and holding views diametrically opposed to those of his father, who was one of the leading Liberals in this City: but he never allowed this difference in politics to interfere with filial duty and affection.

The first political contest in this City in which he took any active part was the election of 1852, when the Liberal candidates were the Right Hon. Milner Gibson and Mr John Bright, the Conservatives Mr George Loch and Captain Denman, the result being that the Conservative candidates were defeated. This led Mr Callender, along with Mr John Sudlow and Mr Maclure, to reorganise the South Lancashire Conservative Association, of which, in 1857, he became chairman for the South-Eastern portion. The various branch associations formed throughout this division of the County under his auspices had the effect, in 1859, of wresting the representation from the Liberals, who had held it uninterruptedly for about twelve years, by returning two Conservatives – the Hon. Algernon Egerton and Mr W. J. Legh. He continued chairman of the association until the Southern portion of the County was divided into South-East and South-West districts, and from then on up to the time of his election or Manchester, he continued to hold that office.

At the General Election of 1868 Mr Callender was strongly pressed to stand in the Conservative interest for the City of Manchester, but in deference to the opinion of his father, who was opposed to it, he declined to contest the borough.

At the last General Election in 1874, an equally unanimous request was presented to him to become a candidate for the representation of this division of the County, but this high honour he waived in favour of Manchester and the offer was made to Mr E. Hardcastle to become coadjutor of the Hon. Algernon Egerton in opposition to Mr P. Rylands and Mr J. E. Taylor, who offered themselves in the Liberal interest. The result was that the two first named gentlemen were returned with an enormous majority. Mr Callender was then asked along with Mr Hugh Birley, the then senior member for this City, to undertake the heavier and more uncertain task of contesting Manchester in the conservative interest against Sir Thomas Bazley and Mr Jacob Bright, who had in the previous Parliament, along with Mr Birley represented the City as the two junior members in the Liberal interest. The struggle was a severe one, but it resulted on the 5th February in placing Mr Birley and Mr Callender at the head of the poll, and the rejection of Mr Jacob Bright. The numbers of voters polled were – Birley, 19,984; Callender, 19,649; Bazley, 19,325; Bright, 18,727. The blow was a terrible one for the Liberals. Manchester had hitherto been considered the head-quarters of the Radical party, and this was the first time that the City had returned two Conservative members, a fact the more significant from their being placed at the head of the poll, Sir Thomas Bazley who had represented the City since 1858, becoming the minority member.

On taking his seat in Parliament, Mr Callender was selected to second the address to the Queen. He did so in an able speech, which elicited marked approval from the leaders of both political parties, Mr Disraeli and Mr Gladstone, as it was delivered with all the aplomb of a finished debater. Later in the session, when the Friendly Societies Bill was under discussion, he strongly opposed the 28th clause, and other clauses which reduced the maximum amount for which a child under five years could be insured from £6 to 30s. And about two months ago a presentation was made to him by the Hulme Conference of Burial Societies for his strenuous and unceasing exertions and the able assistance he rendered them in successfully opposing the objectionable clauses in the Friendly Societies Bill. The impression he made upon the House during his parliamentary career was such that he was spoken of as likely to obtain office, and there is little doubt, had he lived, a baronetcy would have been conferred upon him.

The deceased gentleman, it will be remembered, entertained Mr Disraeli and the late Viscountess Beaconsfield when the present Premier visited Manchester in April, 1872.

Mr Callender was a prominent and highly valued member of the Manchester Athenaeum, and Captain for four years of the Athenaeum Company of Manchester Rifles; he was a leading member of the Masonic fraternity, being Deputy Provincial Grand Master for Lancashire, Grand Deacon of England, and Grand Master of the Mark Masons of England; and he stood in the foremost rank among the supporters of the Masonic and general charities of Manchester. Amongst other offices he held that of deputy-treasurer of the Infirmary, president of the Southern Hospital for the Diseases for Women and Children, and treasurer of the Northern Counties Hospital for Incurables.

He was and active supporter of Owen's college, a trustee of several charities, and in fact he lent a liberal assistance to all societies which provided for the independence and self respect of working men.

He was elected a member of the first Manchester School Board, and was a magistrate and deputy-lieutenant for the County Palatine of Lancaster.

It was undoubtedly in a great measure due to his great powers of organisation and to the formation of the various Conservative Associations throughout that portion of the county, that South Lancashire, from being represented by Liberal members for a series of years, not only in the county but in the boroughs, and from being noted as the most Radical part of the country, came to return Conservative members, and to take the lead in the Defence of the Church of England against her assailants.

As a public speaker he was always exceedingly popular, his speeches being wonderfully clear, full of information and apt illustrations, and always when occasion required, extremely pungent; whilst his kindly and benevolent character rendered him universally esteemed.

The death of Mr Callender was alluded to in several churches in Manchester on Sunday. The Very Rev. the Dean who was morning preacher at the Cathedral, referred to the loss the community had sustained by the removal from their midst of one of the members of Parliament for the City, who was a worthy gentleman and deserving of honour. In the course of a few days the City would no doubt be involved in political strife, and he earnestly hoped that all parties engaged in it would conduct themselves with temperance and moderation.

As soon as the death of Mr Callender became known, the flags at the Town Hall, the Exchange, and other public places were hoisted half-mast high. At the Conservative Club the following communication from Mr J. W. Maclure was posted: - 'Lord Derby has telegraphed to me, expressing his deep regret at the great loss both to the public and to his political friends by the wholly unforeseen fatal termination of Mr Callender's illness, and his sincere sympathy in this heavy bereavement.'

(This was at the end of the obituary.)
Thus the week ends – we follow now the clay;
　　All that was spirit has long passed away:
Can this be death we ask – the answer, No!
　　'Tis but transition!
'Tis but a summons sent
　　To a good soul God lent,
To guide an earthly parliament.

(This follow up was taken from another document)

It was generally thought that, had he lived, a baronetcy would be offered to him in return for his services to Conservatism and charities.

He did not, however, live long enough to enjoy the honour of sitting as member for Manchester. Towards the latter end of 1875 his health broke down, and he was ordered by his medical attendant, Mr Lund, to try the south of France. He left Manchester with this object, but only got as far as London when he became worse. He dared not undertake the sea voyage, and so he was removed to St. Leonards. On Friday, January 21st news reached Manchester that he was better, but the next night a telegram sent anonymously to Mr Maclure announced that Mr Callender was dead. His body was brought home to Manchester, and on the Saturday following, his remains were buried in the churchyard of Heaton Mersey. His funeral was one of the largest that has ever taken place in Manchester and he was followed to the grave by thousands of mourning friends. His companions in Parliament were there, and representatives from all parts of the kingdom. Many Cabinet Ministers wished to be present but were unable to attend.

Mr Callender married, in 1845, Hannah, only daughter of John Mason Esq. and left two sons and three daughters. For the greatest part of his busy life he lived in Victoria Park, Rusholme, and it here he had the honour of entertaining in 1872 the late Earl of Beaconsfield (then Mr Disraeli) and his wife on their visit to Manchester. About three years before his death he removed to Mauldeth Hall, lately the residence of Bishop Lee.

IN MEMORIAM

In manhood's prime, now gathered to his rest,
  The form familiar and the cultured mind;
The generous friend let his past deeds attest,
  That shed the light of mercy on mankind.

Cut off, even in the blossom of his years,
  From honour's path amid the ranks of men;
Long ere the span that circles mortal's fears
  Had measured out its threescore years and ten.

Oft we shall miss him, as each thought endears
  With recollection deep, those scenes again
Of manly rivalry in by-gone years,
  Spent in the sacred cause of duty's reign.

How in the busy marts of commerce fair,
  He strove, in industry and patient zeal,
To exercise aright his talents rare,
  Conducive to the wants of public weal.

Say how he toiled, so steadfast and so true,
  To mitigate the woes of human kind;
And never faltered in that love which grew
  From grace to grace, and ne'er till death declined.

Faithful he walked, and kept his way serene;
  With generous heart stove on from day to day,
While glad benevolence adorned each scene,
  And closed his useful life with peaceful ray.

Thus memory weaves her garlands to his fame,
  And pays her tribute 'mid surrounding gloom;
Thus consecrates his pure and honoured name,
  While all his goodness blossoms o'er his tomb.

Why should we mourn him? For his work is done!
  Yea, rather leave him in the realms of rest;
There virtue triumphs, when life's battle's won,
  Her light shines on, and all her Sons are blest.

APPENDIX VII

RECORDS OF THE FAMILY OF ROMAINE

(I have included these because of the connection between WILLIAM ROMAINE CALLENDER who was my great, great uncle and uncle of my grandfather, Col D.A. CALLENDER.)

This family is of great antiquity, deriving its descent from the early SAXON possessors of the lordship and lands of Romene (near Romney), in Kent, which they retained from the sixth century until the Norman Conquest.

In 616, EUDAF DE ROMENE had embraced Christianity, and procured, in 624, the see of Rochester for one of his sons. Bishop Romene was sent for Justus, Archbishop of Canterbury, with letters to Pope Honorius, but was unfortunately drowned on his passage. Four centuries after, we find the descendants of Eudaf contributing to the success of William the Conqueror, in return for which service they were continued in the possessions of the lands at Romney, and the office of Grand Falconer of England, with the manors of Addington, Ilmere &c. was conferred upon:

ROBERT DE ROMENE, Hereditary Grand Falconer, Grand Sub-feudatory to Odo, Bishop of Bayeux; Lord of the manors of Romenel, Lamport, Addington, Ilmere, &c 1066 to 1080. His son,:

HENRY DE ROMENEL, Grand Falconer, temp, Henry I. was succeeded by,

ROBERT DE ROMENEL, Grand Falconer 1135 to 1146:

DAVID DE ROMENEL, holding his father's office, temp, Henry II had four sons, of whom the third William, succeeded to the representation of the family, after the death of his elder brother; and the youngest, Gabriel, was grandfather of John de Romene, Archbishop of York, Temp, John. David de Romenel's eldest son of:

ROBERT DE ROMENEL had, by his wife Albreda, an only daughter, Albreta, married to William de Jarponville, by which marriage the office of Grand Falconer, and the manors attached to it, passed to the Fitz-Bernards, by arrangement made with:

WILLIAM DE ROMENE, the third son of David. By his wife, Senestria he had:

ROBERT DE ROMENE married Matilda, heiress of John de Hertlepole. His second son:-

JOHN DE ROMEYNE married Alicia, the heiress of Idoworth. His son:

ROBERT DE ROMAYNE married Agnes de B.. He was heir to his uncle Sir Thomas Romayne, Lord Mayor of London, who married the great heiress, Julian de Frennis, niece of Edmund Crouchback, Earl of Lancaster. His son:

WILLIAM DE ROMAYNE enjoyed, in right of his mother, several manors in Berkshire and Dorset, as appears from the visitations in 1377, 1391 and 1399. His son:

ROBERT DE ROMAYNE held the same manors, 1437, temp. Henry II. His son:

JOHN DE ROMAYNE married Isabella de Behmers, by whom he had:

WILLIAM DE ROMAYNE, Lord Lidlinch &c 1453. His son:

JOHN DE ROMAYNE was seised *(authors note: I don't know what this means)* of Lidlinch in 1580, and his son:

HENRY DE ROMAYNE held the manor, temp Edward VI. 1547 to 1553. He was a large merchant and ship owner in London. He was succeeded by:

WILLIAM DE ROMAYNE a merchant in London, temp. Elizabeth. He had three sons of whom:

Nicholas succeeded to the property of Lidlinch &c.

William married Marie Anne daughter of Gabriel de Rigaud, descended from Bernard de Rigaud, living 1697, his son:

Nicholas de Romayne of Rouen and Calais was father

of:

Robert William de Romaine, who succeeded to the representation of the family.

NICHOLAS ROMAYNE, of Strode and Lidlinch died in 1621 and the reversion of Strode descended to his son:

NICHOLAS ROMAYNE, Lieut. In Sir Robert Rich's dragoons and died 17th February 1656, leaving an only son:

NICHOLAS ROMAYNE who married Ann, daughter of Nicholas Fill, and died 7th October 1702, leaving two daughters: ANN, wife of Thomas Derenisk: and PHILLIS, between whom the manors of Lidlinch &c were divided; while the representation of the family devolved on his kinsman:

ROBERT WILLIAM DE ROMAINE, (See above), a merchant of Rouen, who settled in London in 1668. He afterwards removed to Hartlepool and was admitted a burgess of that town in August 1683. His son:

WILLIAM ROMAINE, a merchant and alderman of Hartlepool, born 1672, had, by Isabella his wife, two sons and three daughters, of whom ELIZABETH married MICHAEL CALLENDER, of Newcastle. *(This is where the name of CALLENDER first occurs)* Her eldest son EBENEZER married MARY Potts and had:

WILLIAM ROMAINE CALLENDER, who has issue; of whom the eldest WILLIAM ROMAINE married HANNAH, daughter and co-heiress of John Matson, Esq. and has ARTHUR WILLIAM, JOHN MAYSON, and two daughters.

WILLIAM ROMAINE was succeeded by his second son:

WILLIAM ROMAINE M.A. Rector of St Andrews, by the Wardrobe; and St Ann's Blackfriars. He married 11th February 1755, Mary Price and had two sons, the elder:

WILLIAM ROMAINE, D.D. of Castle Hill, county Berkshire, left two daughters, (NO SONS), his co-heiresses. The younger of whom, Sarah, married the Rev. Robert Gorett, Vicar of Staines, by whom she had eight sons and four daughters. The ROMAINE family name now being extinct, the name and arms were assumed, by Royal license, in 1827, by her second son:

WILLIAM GORETT ROMAINE, C.B Deputy Judge Advocate &c

(Author's note: I am not sure what happened to the Romaine Callender line but it must have something to do with the family.)

APPENDIX VIII

The following wording comes from an original appointment to rank of Ensign in the army of Peter Wright Gent. It is written in brown ink with lots of curly lettering. We understand that, because of his numerous offspring, he couldn't afford to pay for advancement. He was obviously connected to my grandmother's side of the family. (The words in italics were hand written in on the document). It still has its piece of the King's silver.

"George the Third by the Grace of God of the United Kingdom of Great Britain and Ireland. King Defender of the Faith &c. To Our Trusty *and Welbeloved Peter Wright Gent*, Greetings.

We do by these Presents, Constitute and Appoint you to be *Ensign to that Company whereof* (left blank)......*Esq is Captain in Our Sixth (or Royal North British Garrison) Battalion, commanded by Our Trusty and Welbeloved Lieutenant General Paulus Amilius Irving*.

You are therefore carefully and diligently to Discharge the Duty of *Ensign* by Exercising and Well disciplining both the inferior Officers and Soldiers of that *Company* and We do hereby Command them to Obey you as their *Ensign* and You are to observe and follon (*a spelling mistake on the document*) such Orders and Directions from Time to Time as you shall receive from your *Colonel* or any other your superior Officers according to the Rules and Discipline of War on pursuance of the Trust hereby reposed in You. Given at Our Court of *Saint James*, the *Sixteenth* day *of June 1803* in the *forty-third* Year of Our Reign.

Entered with the   *Entered with the Comory*
Secretary at War   *Generals of Musters*
T Moore   *Tho: Butts*

Peter Wright Gent, Ensign in the 6th or Royal North British Invasion Battalion.

APPENDIX IX

Chronological report about the family:

Great grandfather – John Patrick Wright, W.S. Edinburgh Died 1915

Great grandmother – (wife of the above) Jessie Walker Morison, of Falfield, Fife, Died 1932

Their children –
> **Violet Moncrief Lockhart Wright**,
>> Died 1953,
>>> Married Lt Col David Aubrey Callender.
>
> **Winifred**, spinster, died 1903

Their children:
> **Richard Aubrey Callender**, 1901 – January 1987
>
> **Winifred Maud Yolande Nathalie** Callender, 1903 – 1981
>
> **Hyacinth Angela Daphne Callender** 1908 – 1991
>
> **David Ivan Hugo Callender**, 1913-1978

> **Hyacinth Angela Daphne** married,
> Battle, Sussex, 6th August 1954
> Alfred Douglas Holmes – 1896 (London) – 1963
>> (Eastbourne)

Hyacinth Angela Daphne's children:
> **Anna Charlotte Holmes** – 15th September 1942 (London)
> Married (1st) Anton Leslie St John Emmerton – 11th August 1962, Hong Kong

(2nd) Michael Hyde Rains 21st February 1987, Prestbury, Cheshire

Hugo Christopher Holmes – 29th February 1944 (Llandrindod Wells)
Married Victoria Wessell, Leicester

Winifred Elaine Daphne Holmes – 6th September 1946 (Llandrindod Wells)
Married Michael Lake of London, Battle Sussex

Anna's children and grandchildren:
Simon Anton St John – 11 June 1963
Married Anna Stevens – 10th February 1990
Hindon, Wiltshire
Sean Douglas – 13 February 1965
Married Lisa Lindquist – 1989, Laguna Beach, California

Simon's family –
Demelza Moth Emmerton – 20th September 1995

Sean's family –
Hunter McKenzie Sean – 4th July 1991 – Phoenix, Arizona
Grace Marilyn Rose – 13th May 1993 – Stevenage, England
Anton St John Connor – 21st February 1995 – California

Hugo's children and grandchildren:
Robert Douglas - 20th July 1969, Sussex
Married Ouvrielle Roberts, 15 Oct 1994
Benjamin Edward – 22nd January 1972
Married Nev Kalenuik, 12 May 2001

Robert's family – Samuel Hugo Ouvrey Holmes– 21st December 1996
Lucy Alice Holmes– 30th March 1999;
        William Robert Holmes– 18th October 2003

Edward Christopher Holmes– 6th March 2006

Ben's family – Harry Christopher Holmes -13th November 2004

Matthew George (Matty) Holmes – 25th October 2006

Jo's family: Elizabeth (Libby) – 26th October 1980
Libby's family – Georgina Alana Kerry Castle

APPENDIX X

LINEAGE OF ANNA, HUGO AND ELAINE HOLMES
(Through their grandmother's line)

LINEAGE 1

1. Dermot MacMurrough – King of Ireland father of.
2. Princess Eva + Richard de Clare, Earl of Pembroke (the famous 'Strongbow') **(See note below)**
3. Lady Isabel de Clare + William Marshal, who was created Earl of Pembroke in right of his wife.
4. Lady Isabel Marshal + Gilbert de Clare, 1st Earl of Gloucester
5. Lady Isabella de Clare + Robert the Bruce, Lord of Annandale, competitor for the Throne of Scotland against John Baliol
6. Robert the Bruce, Lord Annandale, King of Scotland + Margaret, Countess of Carrick

(Anna, Hugo and Elaine Holmes, 27th in direct line from MacMurrough, King of Ireland.)
Note: The King is said to have solicited aid from King Henry the 2nd of England against his rebellious subjects. Henry sent him Richard de Clare, who rapidly became the most powerful man in Ireland, so much so that MacMurrough is said to have given him his daughter because he feared de Clare would otherwise usurp his Throne – and Henry 2nd himself hurried to Ireland, fearing that de Clare would rival himself.

[For descent from Robert the Bruce, see next lineage]

Notes taken from Google – A Brief History of Ireland

A feud which was to change the fate of Ireland began between two powerful families; Tiernan O'Rourke and Dermot MacMurrough. Two other families joined in as well; Rory O'Connor sided with O'Rourke and Murtogh MacLochlain protected MacMurrough. In 1166 O'Rourke and O'Connor triumphed and chased MacMurrough out of Ireland. MacMurrough was not to be discouraged, however; he returned shortly thereafter with an army provided by Henry II and the assistance of the legendary Richard FitzGilbert de Clare, also known as Strongbow. He eventually managed to take over Ireland and reinstated himself as ruler there. He became sick and died after a short reign, and left his throne to Strongbow. O'Connor and O'Rourke raised an army and attempted to instate MacMurrough's nephew, with whom they sympathized, instead of Strongbow but they were defeated.

Strongbow therefore became King of Ireland, but King Henry had plans of his own. He had provided the army that conquered Ireland, and he wanted Ireland in his empire. So he brought a new army to Ireland, consisting of over 4000 troops. Strongbow surrendered Ireland to him without a drop of blood being shed.

APPENDIX XI

LINEAGE 2

1. Robert the Bruce, King of Scotland + Margaret Countess of Carrick
2. Princess Marjory Bruce + Walter, Baronet Lord High Steward of Scotland
3. King Robert the 2nd + Margaret daughter of Sir Adam Murc
4. Princess Elizabeth Stuart + Sir Thomas Hay, Kt., of Erroll
5. Elizabeth Hay + Sir George Leslie, Kt.
6. Norman Leslie Esq. + Christian , daughter of Sir John Seton
7. George Leslie, 1st Earl of Rothes + Christian, daughter of Walter, Lord Halyburton
8. Hon. Andrew Leslie + Marjory, daughter William, 3rd Earl of Orkney
9. William Leslie, 3rd Earl of Rothes + Margaret, daughter of Sir Michael Balfour (**See note below**)
10. George Leslie, 4th Earl of Rothes + Agnes, daughter of Sir John Somerville
11. Andrew Leslie, 5th Earl of Rothes + Grizel, daughter of Sir James Hamilton
12. Hon. Sir Patrick Leslie + Lady Jean Stewart, daughter of Robert Stewart, Earl of Orkney
13. David Leslie, 1st Lord Newark + Jean, daughter Sir John Yorke, Bt.
14. David Leslie, 2nd Lord Newark – died without surviving male issue and was succeeded by his daughter.
15. Hon. Jean Leslie, Baroness Newark + Sir Alexander Anstruther, Kt161. Hon. Ellan Anstruther +

Rev. John Chalmers D.D.
16. Jane Chalmers + David Walker Esq. of Falfield

17. Bethune James Walker Esq. R.N. + Johanna,
    daughter Rev. George Wright D.D.
24. Anna Jessie Walker + John P Wright Esq. W.S.
25. Violet Wright + Col. David Callender
26. Daphne Callender + Alfred Douglas Holmes
27. Anna, Hugo and Elaine Holmes

Note:
William Leslie, 3rd Earl of Rothes was younger brother of George 2nd Earl who died unmarried.
William, 3rd Earl, George 2nd Earl and Sir Michael Balfour, father of the 3rd Earl were all killed at Flodden and it is a disputed point whether William was ever 3rd Earl or whether or not he died before his brother the 2nd Earl.

APPENDIX XII

LINEAGE 3

1. William the Conqueror – father of :-
2. Princess Gundred (youngest daughter) + William of Warrenne, 1st Earl of Surry, so created by 'The Conqueror' after the Battle of Hastings.
3. William de Warrenne, 2nd Earl of Surrey + Isabella, daughter of Hugh, Count of Vermandois, son of Henri the 1st, King of France
4. Lady Adela de Warrenne + Henry, Prince of Scotland, eldest son of David the 1st, King of Scotland
5. David, Earl of Huntingdon, (3rd son) + Maud, daughter of Hugh, Earl of Chester
6. Lady Isabel le Scot + Robert the Bruce, Lord of Annandale
7. Robert the Bruce, Lord of Annandale + Margaret, Countess of Carrick

Note:

Daphne Callender: 28th from William the Conqueror
28th from Henri the 1st King of France
26th from David 1st of Scotland

David, Earl of Huntingdon, was younger brother of Malcolm the 4th and William the Lion, Kings of Scotland

APPENDIX XIII

LINEAGE 4

1. King Robert the 2nd – father of
2. Princess Egidia Stuart + William Douglas, Lord of Nithsdale **(See note below)**
3. Hon. Egidia Douglas + Henry St Clair, 2nd Earl of Orkney
4. William St Clair, 3rd Earl of Orkney + (2nd wife) Marjory Sutherland **(See note below)**
5. Lady Marjory St Clair + Hon. Andrew Leslie
6. William Leslie, 3rd Earl of Rothes + Margaret, daughter of Sir Michael Balfour. **(See note below)**
7. George Leslie, 4th Earl of Rothes + Agnes, daughter of Sir John Somerville
8. Andrew Leslie, 5th Earl of Rothes + Grizel, daughter of Sir James Hamilton
9. Hon. Sir Patrick Leslie + Lady Jean Stewart, daughter Robert Earl of Orkney
10. David Leslie, 1st Lord Newark – ancestor of – Daphne Callender – 17th from Robert the 2nd

Notes:

1. There seems to be two different spellings for the daughter of King Robert 2nd. On one of the lists compiled by Richard Callender, my mother's elder brother it calls her Princess Egidia and on the other, Princess Elizabeth. I don't know which is correct.

2. William St Clair, 3rd Earl of Orkney, was compelled to surrender his Earldom of Orkney to James the 3rd

and the Earldom was annexed to the Crown by Act of Parliament. In compensation he was granted several Estates and created Earl of Caithness.

3. Her brother, who should have been 4th Earl of Orkney married Lady Christian Leslie, her husband's sister.

APPENDIX XIV

LINEAGE OF ANNA, HUGO AND ELAINE HOLMES TO THE ROYAL HOUSE OF STEWART,

Through their grandfather's line

1. James I, Kings of Scots + Joan Beaufort, descended from Edward III
2. James II + Mary Gueldres
3. James III + Margaret of Denmark
4. James IV + Margaret Drummond
5. Lady Katharine Stewart + James, 3rd Earl of Morton
6. Lady Beatrix Douglas + Robert, 6th Lord Maxwell
7. John 8th Lord Maxwell (created Earl of Morton on the execution of Regent Morton) + Lady Elizabeth Douglas daughter of 7th Earl of Angus
8. Lady Elizabeth Maxwell, sister of 1st Earl of Nithsdale
    + John Maxwell, 6th Lord Herries, died 1631
9. James Maxwell of Breckonside, Dumfries-shire 2nd son + Margaret Vans of Barnbarrow and widow of Sir John Gordon
10. Alexander Maxwell of Terraughtie + Margaret, daughter and co-heir of Alexander Murray of Terraughtie
11. John Maxwell of Terraughtie, d. 12 May 1724 + wife
12. John Maxwell of Munches and Terraughtie, served heir male of Earl of Nithsdale + wife
13. Jean Maxwell, d. 10 July 1815 + William Hyslop of Lochend
14. Agnes Hyslop + David Gordon, 3rd son of Sir

Alexander Gordon of Culvennan
15. Grace Gordon + Charles Potter of Earnsdale, Lancs
16. Agnes Potter + Samuel Pope Callender
17. Col. David Callender + Violet Wright
18. Hyacinth Angela Daphne + Alfred Douglas Holmes
19. Anna, Hugo and Elaine

APPENDIX XV

LINEAGE OF THE GORDON'S
AND THE LOCHINVARS.

(The line of Col. David Callender)

SIR ADAM DE GORDOUN, 1st Lord of Lochinvar, the friend and companion in arms of SIR WILLIAM WALLACE, Charter of Glenkens, Kenmure and Lochinvar, 1297, Ambassador to the Pope, 1305. Received from Edward II the Manor of Stitchel, 1309. Died 1330.

Sir WILLIAM DE GORDOUN, of Stitchel, 2nd Lord of Lochinvar. Ob. 1360

ROGER DE GORDOUN, of Stitchel, 3rd Lord of Lochinvar (Le Sire de Gordoun, killed at Homildon Hill, September 14, 1402).

Sir ALEXANDER DE GORDON, of Stitchel, 4th Lord of Lochinvar. Gets a Charter of Glenkens, 1410. Ob. 1420

ROGER DE GORDON, of Stitchel, 5th Lord of Lochinvar. Gets Charter of Balmaclellan, 1422. Ob. 1442

WILLIAM DE GORDON, of Stitchel, 6th Lord of Lochinvar. Ob 1490. He was the 'Young Lochinvar' of Lady Heron's song in 'Marmion'.

ALEXANDER GORDON, of Auchenreoch. Second son the above WILLIAM GORDON, Lord of Lochinvar

ALEXANDER GORDON, of Airds. Married MARGARET SINCLAIR, of Earlstoun. Ob. 1580, aged 101.

JOHN GORDON, of Airds. Married ELIZABETH GORDON, of Blacket. Ob. 1606

JOHN GORDON, of Earlstoun. Married, 1st, MARGARET SINCLAIR, heiress of Earlstoun; 2nd, M. CHALMERS, of Gadgirth. Ob. 1628

ALEXANDER GORDON, of Earlstoun. Married ELIZABETH GORDON, of Penninghame. Ob. 1653

WILLIAM GORDON, of Earlstoun. Married MARY HOPE, of Graighall. Killed at Bothwell Bridge. 1679.

Sir WILLIAM GORDON, of Afton (younger son). Created Baronet, 1706, for military services of distinction. 1st Baronet. Landed at Torbay with William of Orange. Married MARY CAMPBELL, daughter of Sir GEORGE CAMPBELL, of Cessnock, sister of the COUNTESS OF MARCHMONT, but died without issue and was succeeded by his elder brother.

ALEXANDER GORDON, Bart., of Earlstoun, who after the battle of Bothwell Bridge 1679, (where his father, WILLIAM GORDON, of Earlstoun, was killed), was captured and sentenced to be beheaded 20th August, 1683, but remained a prisoner at Edinburgh Castle, the Bass Rock and Blackness Castle for six years. He married, first, JANET, the daughter of Sir THOMAS HAMILTON of Preston, Baronet, from which union descended PATRICIA GORDON, the granddaughter of the marriage, the mother of LORD PANMURE, Minister of War 1856; and also Sir WILLIAM GORDON, the 6th Baronet of Earlstoun, Member of the Legion of Honour, Captain in the 17th Lancers, who was much wounded in the desperate charge of the Light Cavalry at Balaclava.

Sir CHARLES GORDON, 7th Baronet – a cousin of the late Sir WILLIAM – now represents this first marriage.

Sir ALEXANDER GORDON married secondly, the HONOURABLE MARION GORDON, Daughter of ALEXANDER GORDON, 5th VISCOUNT KENMURE and 16th Lord of Lochinvar: and their son, WILLIAM GORDON of Greenlaw, county of Kirkcudbright, married ISABELL McCULLOCH GORDON, daughter of the FOURTH GORDON of Culvennan, in Wigtonshire, who were the descendants of WILLIAM GORDON, of Craig-Lammington, his spouse, son of Sir ROBERT GORDON, 8th Lord Lochinvar.

Their son, Sir ALEXANDER GORDON, of Culvennan and Greenlaw, Kt., Sheriff of Wigton, married GRACE DALRYMPLE, sister of Sir JOHN DALRUMPLE HAY, Baronet, county of Wigton.

Their second son, DAVID GORDON, married AGNES HYSLOP, granddaughter of JOHN HERRIES MAXWELL, of Terraughtie and Munches, the representative of the noble house of Nithsdale; for he was, 4th June, 1778, served heir-male to ROBERT, FOURTH EARL of Nithsdale: who was attainted on Tower Hill: but his Countess effected his escape.

DAVID GORDON married AGNES HYSLOP
(Six children)

GRACE GORDON, daughter married CHARLES POTTER of Earnsdale, Lancs. (Two children)

AGNES POTTER, daughter, married SAMUEL CALLENDER (10 children) **(See note below)**
DAVID CALLENDER, (7th son) married VIOLET WRIGHT, (4 children)

RICHARD CALLENDER (no issue)

NATHALIE CALLENDER (unmarried – no issue)

HYACINTH ANGELA DAPHNE CALLENDER married ALFRED DOUGLAS HOLMES (3 children)

HUGO CALLENDER (1 son)

ANNA CHARLOTTE HOLMES (daughter) married ANTON EMMERTON (2 sons) – Simon and Sean

HUGO CHRISTOPHER HOLMES (son) married VICTORIA WESSEL (2 sons) – Robert and Ben
WINIFRED ELAINE DAPHNE HOLMES (daughter) married MICHAEL LAKE (1daughter) Elizabeth
Note:
W R CALLENDER Esq. married HANNAH POPE, daughter of SAMUEL POPE Esq. of Exeter
WILLIAM ROMAINE CALLENDER MP (Born in Manchester 1825 d. 1876. Eldest son
SAMUEL CALLENDER, brother of William Romaine, married AGNES POTTER (See above)

ABOUT THE AUTHOR

The author, Anna Rains, moved for the forty-eighth time in 2006, having previously lived in England, Scotland, Wales, Hong Kong and California. She has experienced every conceivable type of home: a bus after the Second World War, a caravan, a 120-foot schooner in Hong Kong, a houseboat on the Birdham Canal near Chichester, skyscrapers, high rises, town houses, a thatched cottage and a haunted Cheshire farmhouse.

For the past twenty-five years, she has lived in Cheshire, near Macclesfield, where she has been involved in fundraising for local charities, doing Punch and Judy shows and speaking to the local Women's Institutes about ghosts and fortune-telling, as well as returning, soon after her sixty-fifth birthday, to work as a part-time training officer for a large firm of Estate Agents.

She has had almost as many careers as she has had living quarters. Apart from training sales staff, she has worked in the hotel industry, travel, selling high-priced watches in Hong Kong, and as a telephonist and typist in England. Other ventures have been in Real Estate, as 'short-order' cook in a café, in banking, motivational sales, boat sales and sales of coffins and caskets, all in California before she came back to England to start her own business as a Sales Trainer.

Anna comes from a family that can be traced back in direct line to William the Conqueror. She has many other illustrious ancestors, many of them very eccentric, particularly her more recent nearest relatives. As one after another of the older members of her family died, she decided she had to put some of the most memorable stories down on paper so that her grandchildren and future great-grandchildren would know all about their forebears – otherwise the stories would be lost.

Lightning Source UK Ltd.
Milton Keynes UK
28 September 2009

144274UK00002B/36/P